D1274197

WITHDRAWN

Steven F. White, Editor

POETS OF NICARAGUA

A Bilingual Anthology, 1918~1979

INTRODUCTION BY GRACE SCHULMAN

GREENSBORO: UNICORN PRESS 1982

Translation copyright © Steven F. White, 1982

Introduction copyright © Grace Shulman, 1982

The woodblock by Pablo Antonio Cuadra is reproduced by permission of Unicorn Press, Inc. All rights reserved.

Library of Congress Cataloging in Publication Data
Main entry under title:
Poets of Nicaragua, a bilingual anthology, 1918-1979.
 Poems in Spanish; with English translations by S.F. White
 Bibliography: p. 203-208
 Contents: Alfonso Cortés—Salomón de la Selva—José Coronel Urtecho—[etc.]
  1. Nicaraguan poetry—20th century—Translations into English. 2. English poetry—Translations from Spanish. 3. Nicaraguan poetry—20th century. I. White, Steven F., 1955-
PO7516.5.E5P6   861   81-23093

ISBN 0-87775-132-3 *cloth*
ISBN 0-87775-133-1 *paper*

The translator was aided in his work in Nicaragua by the Hubbard Hutchinson Fellowship granted to him by Williams College.

Assistance in the publication of this book was given by the Center for Inter-American Cultural Relations

Grateful acknowledgement is made by Unicorn Press to the following poets, publishers and literary executors to reprint the poems in this volume in their original language:

ALFONSO CORTÉS with permission of the poet's sister, Maria Luisa Cortés, literary executor;

SALOMÓN DE LA SELVA with the permission of the poet's son, Salomón de la Selva Castrillo, literary executor;

PABLO ANTONIO CUADRA with the poet's personal permission and with those, for previously published poems, of Carlos Lohlé, Buenos Aires, Argentina (*El jaguar y la luna*), copyright 1971, and Ediciones Academia Nicaragüense, Managua, Nicaragua (*Cantos de Cifar y la mar dulce*), copyright 1979;

JOAQUIN PASOS with the permission of the poet's brother, Luis Pasos, literary executor.

Personal permission has been given by the following poets; by whom all rights are reserved: ERNESTO CARDENAL, JOSÉ CORONEL URTECHO, JUAN FRANCISCO GUTIÉRREZ, ERNESTO MEJÍA SÁNCHEZ, CARLOS MARTÍNEZ RIVAS, ERNESTO GUTIÉRREZ, FRANCISCO VALLE, ANA ILCE, and ÁLVARO URTECHO.

THE TRANSLATOR DEDICATES HIS WORK TO THE NEW NICARAGUA

"... pues tú eres la crisálida de mi alma entristecida,
y te he de ver en medio del triunfo que merezcas,
renovando el fulgor de mi psique abolida."

Rubén Darío

ERRATA

Page	For	Read
ii, line 24	Somozo	Somoza
21, line 6	live.	life.
58, Title	Damien	Damian
59, line 1	Alcahualinc	Alcahualinca
65, line 11	indians	Indians
69, line 13	indian	Indian
120, line 21	es	en
125, line 10	bolden	golden
129, line 26	death	flesh
145, line 25	come	comes

Table of Contents

Ernesto Gutiérrez

Francisco Valle

Ana Ilce

Álvaro Urtecho

* Written originally in English

INTRODUCTION

Poetry of a New Heaven and Earth

Although this anthology begins, appropriately, after the work of Rubén Darío, the profound influence he exerted on Nicaraguan writing, and on all of Spanish literature, is felt to this day. In fact, in contemporary letters, Nicaragua is best known as the birthplace of Darío who, as leader of *modernismo,* or the Modernist movement, freed Spanish poetry in Spain and Latin America from prosaic dullness. A poet-diplomat who lived for many years in France, Spain and in other South American countries, Rubén Darío was, at the same time, bound fast to his native country, having spent his first seventeen years there and having returned there to die.

As early as 1888, Rubén Darío's *Azul,* a slim volume of prose and poetry, caught the attention of Spanish critics and lifted the domination of uninspired nineteenth-century verse. His poetry, influenced by the French Parnassians and by the symbolists, is marked by luminous, magical images that are precise and yet suggestive of a remote, hidden radiance. His vision of essential splendor and his ideal of perfect music are derived from Poe. And, although his metaphors referred commonplace things to a realm of ethereal elegance, he did, like Walt Whitman, whom he admired, create a poetry of real things and ordinary objects—the spider, the toad, the crab—blazing new ways of using the imaginative faculty to elevate common experience. And, in such poems as "Far Away and Long Ago," he creates wonder in the landscape of Nicaragua—the flaming sun, the ox, the pigeon, the farm, the dove—all things that remain fundamental to his very being.

At the time of Rubén Darío's death in 1916, there were growing reactions against his poetry, and against the Modernist movement. In Nicaragua, the trio of post-Modernists included Alfonso Cortés,

i

Salomón de la Selva and Azarías Pallais. Cortés and de la Selva, both represented here, departed from the intricate imagery and elevated diction of Modernism, Cortés finding a way into his own mysterious, inner being, and de la Selva turning outward, creating a poetry of deep concern for human suffering.

The Nicaraguan literary Vanguard, a movement dedicated to renewing the country's writing, was inaugurated in 1927 by José Coronel Urtecho, and included Pablo Antonio Cuadra and Joaquín Pasos. Although the styles of those writers varied considerably, they were alike in the wish to create a literature free from European domination, which was to be an aesthetic counterpart of the political desire to liberate Nicaragua from foreign intervention.

The Vanguard began when José Coronel Urtecho returned from the United States in 1927 and gathered together a group of students dedicated to an autonomous Nicaragua. Like Salomón de la Selva who had, a decade before, given radical lectures in the United States, the young students were deeply humiliated by the presence of the American Marines, who were stationed in Nicaragua for seventeen years. The group was inspired by Augusto César Sandino, the guerilla fighter who continued his warfare in the northern mountains until the Marines were withdrawn in 1933. The Vanguard's aims were political as well as aesthetic: naively, they sought to educate the people to provide for their welfare by providing a benevolent leader in the person of General Anastasio Somozo, who later persecuted many of those same writers.

In poetry, the Vanguard's rebellion had far happier results: the group wanted a poetry indigenous to Nicaragua, and free from the formal, European conventions that Modernism had imposed. Author of "Ode to Rubén Darío," José Coronel conceived the Vanguard as furthering the literary freedom that the Nicaraguan master had initiated; at the same time, he called for a departure from Darío's ornamentation and a freer use of form. José Coronel, who translated poems by Marianne Moore and Ezra Pound into Spanish, is a superb teacher, critic and conversationalist. His own work is experimental: his innovative rhythms are patterned by received forms as well as popular dance tunes, and he exhibits a great range of tone, from gently mocking humor to deep seriousness. Joaquín Pasos, the youngest member of the Vanguard who died at the age of thirty-three, creates a poetry of an interior landscape that also embodies the indigenous inner life of his people.

The initial book of poetry from the Nicaraguan literary Vanguard, *Poemas nicaragüenses (Nicaraguan Poems)*, was written by Pablo Antonio Cuadra, and appeared in 1934 when the poet was twenty-two years old. The book heralded a rebirth of his country's people, for it celebrated Nicaraguan customs, villages, farms and people. After his active political period, and his disillusionment with the elder Somoza, Cuadra went through a severe spiritual crisis that was reflected in *Canto Temporal (Temporal Song)*. Of that inner conflict, he wrote: "I used to have faith in the Faith—but this decisive encounter with Christ revealed to me faith in love." In *Cantos de Cifar (Songs of Cifar)*, he writes of the people he has lived and worked among: the sailors who dry their nets in the sun, the fishermen who smell the smoke of breakfast, the merchants, the owners of sailboats, the sailors who row in gentle winds and in storms, insulting the rain and the waves. Using a vocabulary that is plain and yet elevated to an epic tone, Cuadra creates the character of Cifar, a sailor who sees Lake Nicaragua as an organic part of the soul, a seeing speaker close to the *periplum* of Pound's *The Cantos,* and to the speaker of Whitman's *Leaves of Grass* who identifies with every leaf, star and atom.

Ernesto Cardenal is, along with Ernesto Mejía Sánchez and Carlos Martínez Rivas, one of the chief poets who came into artistic power in the nineteen-forties. The most socially committed *and* contemplative of the Nicaraguan Vanguard, deeply concerned with the plight of the common people, Cardenal has believed that poetry should be at the service of political change. A poet, priest and revolutionary, Ernesto Cardenal founded a community to serve the poor on the Island of Solentiname. The colony was dispersed but, after the revolution of 1979, Cardenal became Minister of Culture. Cardenal envisions a poetry of a wider American tradition and, in his own work, makes original use of Whitman and Ezra Pound when he looks closely at the beauty of natural things and regards the wonders of urban life. Unique to Cardenal, though, are the pressing concerns, simultaneously, with human brutality and with the indissoluble ties between God and humankind.

Carlos Martínez Rivas, author of a powerful book of poetry, *La Insurrección Solitaria,* is, like Cardenal, at once contemplative and profoundly aware of human destruction. Whether writing of religious legends or of social realities, he concentrates always on the single human action on which the event depends. He casts a cold eye on all worldly experience, perceiving matters in minute detail and with remote compassion. In "Saint Christopher," it is the child who hears nothing but "the rain / falling in the abyss," and in "Kiss for Lot's Wife" the speaker observes "a woman recognizes her king / even when nations tremble and the skies rain fire."

Of the new poets represented in this anthology, Ana Ilce is an example of the many women poets who have emerged in Nicaragua in the past decade, and especially since the revolution of 1979. Although her love poems are keenly felt, they have a sense of distance and essential solitude; the people in her poetic world are real, but they live at the border of a region that is remote and even abstract. Like many of her contemporaries, she is hardly concerned with the social realism or the religious quest that engaged her precursors. Instead, she writes freely of natural things, at once alive to the world and aware of a hidden beauty beyond it.

It is a commonplace that artists have, throughout history, done their true work regardless of political crises and religious dilemmas. This seems especially true of the poets of Nicaragua, who have either confronted social realities or glanced beyond them, temporarily at least, depending on the exigencies of their work at the time. Pablo Antonio Cuadra, for many years co-director of *La Prensa* and Director of *La Prensa Literaria,* wrote an influential newspaper column called "Escrito a Máquina" ("Typewritten") to separate his thoughts on national matters from his poems, which he wrote in longhand. It was one of the many indications of his double vision of human concern and aesthetic commitment

Once I asked him why, during the revolutionary siege of 1979, he continued to send me poems about the trees he loved and about the lucidity of Lake Nicaragua even in answer to my inquiries about his safety and well-being. "How could you write those beautiful poems about ceiba trees when your city was burning?" I asked. "What else is a man to do?" he replied.

The work of making English versions of Nicaraguan poems has something of the same urgency. There is a compelling need to convey those poems regardless of social, political or religious realities. Thomas Merton, who was Director of Novitiates at the Abbey of Gethsemani, in Kentucky, when Ernesto Cardenal was a novitiate there, introduced the world of Cardenal, Cortés and Cuadra to English-speaking readers. Monique and Carlos Altschul, who lived in Argentina, worked closely with Cardenal in translating his work into English. And for the present volume, translator Steven White, shortly after his graduation from Williams College, worked on a coffee farm in Northern Nicaragua to experience the culture firsthand and to learn of the divergences of the country's Spanish. Then, in the course of selecting and studying the poems, he worked intimately with the poets—even on the eve of the revolution of 1979—to avoid errors and textual misunderstandings.

Although translation of Nicaraguan poetry into English is still in its infancy, it does signify a glorious birth. The poems are alive with spiritual force, erotic power and transcendent beauty. They sing of a wider American tradition, one that encompasses vast areas of space and the wonders of common things. They resonate with a vitality that comes only with the dread knowledge of loneliness, despair and death.

Grace Schulman

To enter the city of Nicaraguan poetry one must first pass the landmark that guards the gates—Rubén Darío. I remember my Spanish teacher in high school trying to convince an unreceptive class that one could actually hear the trumpets and drums in "Marcha triunfal". In college, during a night of wine, my good friend from Nicaragua recited "Lo fatal". I was amazed. He then told me that on the same fields where I was playing soccer, another poet from his country, Salomón de la Selva, had practiced drills in preparation for World War I.

After a year in Ecuador, Peru and Chile working with poets and learning to dream, as well as speak, in Spanish, I read Darío's "A Roosevelt", looked at the newspapers, and decided that Nicaragua was where I had to be. When I arrived in Managua, the streets were filled with people demonstrating against Somoza on the first anniversary of the murder of Pedro Joaquín Chamorro. Considering that period of Nicaraguan history, it was appropriate that my friend took me on my first day to the active volcano near Masaya called *La Boca del Infierno*.

Working on a coffee farm outside of Matagalpa for two months, until the end of the harvest, accustomed me to Nicaraguan Spanish. I felt ready to begin my translating project. But because books were difficult to find even in the capital, I traveled from city to city meeting many poets and going over my translations with them. I could not have accomplished anything without the incredible help and hospitality I received during my stay. I left Nicaragua at the end of May, 1979 and continued my work in Costa Rica until the Sandinista victory in July.

The events that preceded this historic moment made it very diffi cult for me to cast a cold eye on everything I read during the process of selecting the poetry for this book. Nevertheless, the result is not a collection of verse whose sole purpose is to bear witness to injustice and terror. Nor, in its brevity, can the selection be called comprehensive. This limited anthology, however, reverses the flow of the cultural imperialism that has inundated Nicaragua and shows us, the people of the United States, the face of a country that has stood up to the oppressive forces of our times. Cultural dialogue between the Americas will prove that this tiny land has more to export than coffee, cotton and cattle. It is fitting that Nicaragua has produced literary riches that equal and even surpass those of larger and more developed countries.

Steven F. White

POETS OF NICARAGUA

A Bilingual Anthology, 1918–1979

Alfonso Cortés
(1893-1969)

Two of Nicaragua's greatest poets lived in the same house and are buried side by side in the cathedral of León. Cortés spent much of his life in the house on the *Calle Real* where Rubén Darío had lived as a boy. The Nicaraguans call Cortés *"El Poeta Loco"* but insist that, although he lost his reason and was prone to fits of violence that coincided with the full moon, he never lost his ability to create poetry. Cortés went insane, according to his sisters, on February 18, 1927 at midnight and in the ensuing years wrote some of his best poetry while he was chained to a wall by a window. Many of these poems are written on pieces of paper the size of cigarette packages in microscopic letters. His poetry flashes with the enigmas of the Romantics and Symbolists. Among his papers, Cortés left translations of Baudelaire, Verlaine, Mallarmé, D'Annunzio and Poe. José Coronel calls the mysterious, prophetic poetry of Cortés *la poesía alfonsina* to distinguish it from the great body of Cortés' work that is simply bad writing. The *poesía alfonsina* is a metaphysical poetry concerned with Space, Time, Being, God, Form and Matter. These poems are like great bolts of lightning divorced from any kind of temporal context. In Cortés's song of internal space, the poet wanders in a world of imagination and dream.

LA CANCIÓN DEL ESPACIO

La distancia que hay de aquí a
una estrella que nunca ha existido
porque Dios no ha alcanzado a
pellizcar tan lejos la piel de la
noche! Y pensar que todavía creamos
que es más grande o más
útil la paz mundial que la paz
de un solo salvaje...

Este afán de relatividad de
nuestra vida contemporánea —es—
lo que da al espacio una importancia
que sólo está en nosotros, —
y quién sabe hasta cuándo aprenderemos
a vivir como los astros —
libres en medio de lo que es sin fin
y sin que nadie nos alimente.

La tierra no conoce los caminos
por donde a diario anda —y
más bien esos caminos son la
conciencia de la tierra... —Pero si
no es así, permítaseme hacer una
pregunta: —Tiempo, dónde estamos
tú y yo, yo que vivo en tí y
tú que no existes?

THE SONG OF SPACE

The distance from here to
a star that never existed
because God has not succeeded in
stretching the night's skin
that far! And to think we still believe
that world peace is more
useful, greater, and comes before
the peace of a single savage . . .

This fascination with relativity
in our contemporary life: that's
what gives space an importance
found only in ourselves.
And who knows when we'll learn
to live like the stars—
free admidst all that has no end
and needing no one to feed us.

The earth does not know the roads
where it journeys every day.
Yet those roads are the
earth's awareness . . . But allow me
a question if this is not so:
Time, where are we,
you and I, since I live in you
and you do not exist?

EL BARCO PENSATIVO

En la sonante playa, con ímpetu afanoso
    y movimiento vivo,
tiende sus velas tristes al viento poderoso
    el barco pensativo.

Es el hombre. Sus sueños, como marinos graves
    van en callada tropa;
mujeres siempre bellas y trémulas como aves
    se sientan en la popa.

La incógnita esperanza, petrel de largo vuelo,
    en los mástiles ronda
y un coro de recuerdos, coronados de cielo,
    se aleja sobre la onda.

Vienen del puente voces, se ordena y se trabaja
    bajo las ciudadelas
estáticas de éter; mientras el viento ultraja
    el telón de las velas.

El sol imprime exámetros de plata en las espumas,
    en el azul se lanza
una ciudad de luces y de brumas;
    el horizonte danza.

Y el Capitán, en tanto que la visión celeste
    de la hora se disipa,
se acerca a una alta verga y ve alejarse al Este
    el humo de su pipa.

THE PENSIVE SHIP

Where the waves roar,
the pensive ship spreads its sails
of sadness to the wind
and struggles to embark.

Like solemn sailors, its dreams
journey in silent ranks.
Trembling, ever-beautiful women
sit like birds in the stern.

A seagull, like some unknown hope,
circles the masts and memory
sings with a crown of sky
above the distant whitecaps.

Voices from the bridge! They give orders
to work beneath the blue fortress
locked in space as the wind
buffets the canvas of the sails.

The sun engraves a poem
of silver on the waves.
A city of light and mist
dances on the horizon.

While the hour's celestial vision
dissolves, the Captain
leans on a high spar and sees
smoke from his pipe recede in the East.

LAS TRES HERMANAS

Hada es la luz, Estela la armonía,
y Teresa la gracia. Y en Teresa,
en Estela y en Hada, culmina esa
fiesta de amor que hace perfecto el día.

Una canta. Otra sueña. Otra confía
al tiempo errante su ilusión ilesa,
y en la sonrisa de las tres se expresa
la suprema verdad de la poesía.

Las tres hermanas en felices horas,
hilan en ruecas de ilusión sus vidas,
como la encarnación de tres auroras

gemelas, y en sus danzas y sus juegos,
van hacia la Esperanza, precedidas
por un coro feliz de niños ciegos.

THE THREE SISTERS

Hada is light, Estela is harmony
and Theresa is grace. And from Theresa,
Estela and Hada emanates that
feast of love that fulfills the day.

One sings. Another dreams. Another confides
to errant time her unscathed illusions,
and the smile of the three reveals
the supreme truth of poetry.

The three sisters in joyful hours
spin their lives on distaffs of imagination
like the incarnation of triplet

dawns. And in their dances and games
they move toward hope, preceded
by a happy chorus of blind children.

IRREVOCABLEMENTE

Por donde quiera que escudriña la mirada,
sólo encuentra los pálidos pantanos de la Nada;
flores marchitas, aves sin rumbo, nubes muertas...
Ya no abrió nunca el cielo ni la tierra sus puertas!
Días de lasitud, desesperanza y tedio;
no hay más para la vida que el fúnebre remedio
de la muerte, no hay más!, no hay más!, no hay más
que caer como un punto negro y vago
en la onda lívida del lago,
para siempre jamás...

IRREVOCABLY

Wherever the gaze finally comes to rest,
it finds only pale swamps of Nothingness,
dead clouds, birds without bearing, withered flowers...
Both earth and sky have closed their doors!
Days of lassitude, hopelessness, tedium—
nothing more for life but the funereal remedy
of death, nothing more, nothing more, nothing more
except to fall like a point, black and vague,
on the livid wave of the lake
forever and ever.

FUGA DE OTOÑO

Aquí todo, hasta el tiempo se hace espacio. En los viejos
caminos nuestra voz yerra como un olvido,
y a un éter lleno de recuerdos, se ha salido
de nosotros el alma, para vernos de lejos.

El cielo es como un fiel recuerdo de colores,
en que tú arremolinas, luz sonora, tus vientos;
la loca de la tarde hunde sus pensamientos
de luz, en la epidermis de seda de las flores.

Yo hilaré con el blanco vellón de los vesperos,
horas de amor sutiles, concisas y espaciosas
viendo venir las pálidas parejas amorosas
en la convalescencia feliz de los senderos.

FLIGHT OF AUTUMN

Everything here, even time, becomes space.
Our voice wanders the old roads like something forgotten
and our soul has gone to a sky crowded with memories
to watch us from a distance.

The sky is a faithful memory of colors
where a resonant wind swirls in the afternoon
like a madwoman sinking
her thoughts in the silken skin of flowers.

With the white fleece of the first stars
I will spin the hours of love, spacious and delicate,
when I see the pale lovers descend
the glad convalescence of the paths.

LA DANZA DE LOS ASTROS

La sombra azul y vasta es un perpetuo vuelo
que estremece el inmóvil movimiento del cielo;
la distancia es silencio, la visión es sonido;
el alma se nos vuelve como un místico oído
en que tienen las formas propia sonoridad;
luz antigua en sollozos estremece el Abismo,
y el Silencio Nocturno se levanta en sí mismo.
Los violines del éter pulsan su claridad.

THE DANCE OF THE STARS

The vast blue shadow is a perpetual flight
that shakes the sky's motionless movement at night;
distance is silence, vision is sound,
the soul like a mystic ear, selfward bound,
where all forms have their own sonority;
an ancient sobbing light shakes the Abyss,
inside itself the Nocturnal Silence lifts.
The violins of ether throb their clarity.

YO

Muchos me han dicho: —El viento, el mar, la lluvia, el grito
de los pastores…Otros: —La hembra humana y el cielo;
otros: —La errante sombra y el invisible velo
de la Verdad, y aquellos: —La fantasía, el mito.

Yo no. Yo sé que todo es inefable rito
en el que oficia un coro de arcángeles en vuelo,
y que la eternidad vive en sagrado celo,
en el que engendra el Hombre y pare lo infinito.

Por eso, mis palabras son silencio hablado,
y en la fatal urdimbre de cada ser, encuentro
difícil lo sabido y fácil lo ignorado…

Yo soy el Mercader de una divina feria
en la que el infinito es círculo sin centro
y el número la forma de lo que es materia.

I

Many have told me, "The wind, the sea,
the rain, the shepherds' cry."
Others, "Woman and sky."
Others, "The wandering shadow
and the invisible veil of truth."
And still others, "Fantasy, myth."

Not for me. I know everything is an ineffable
ritual sung by archangels in the sky.
I know eternity lives with a sacred fervor
where mankind procreates and gives birth to infinity.

That is why my words are spoken silence
and why, in the mortal warp of every human,
I find the known difficult, easy the overlooked.

I am the merchant at a divine fair
where a circle with no center is infinity
and the form of matter is a number.

PASOS

Cuando, en el tumulto de la Tierra,
sientan los seres su soledad,
dará una tregua eterna la guerra
del Ruido; hundirá en la antigüedad

sus pasos el Hombre y la Mujer,
surcarán la arruga de la frente
de Dios, donde del éxtasis de Ayer
se alza vapor incesantemente...

Y quedarán los enamorados
—como despiertos— y dos a dos,
la mirada fija en los Sagrados
Poros, de eterno sudor bañados,
de la frente arrugada de Dios!

STEPS

When we feel our solitude
in the Earth's tumult,
Clamor will end its war and declare
an eternal truce. Men and women

will sink their steps in ancient times
and plough the wrinkles on God's
forehead where mist rises without end
from the ecstasy of the Past.

And as if they were awake,
the lovers will fix their eyes on the Sacred
Pores bathed in eternal sweat
from the furrowed brow of God!

MISERERE

Señor, jamás mis manos manché en viles oficios
aunque las ha quemado la fiebre de los vicios;
maniaté mis corderos para tus sacrificios.

Señor, mis pobres ojos con miradas impuras,
se pierden por los dédalos de mis sendas oscuras,
pero siempre que puedo los vuelvo a tus alturas.

Señor, en vano afino mís oídos rendidos,
por escuchar el canto de tu voz. Mis oídos
solo escuchan gemidos, gemidos y gemidos.

MISERERE

Lord, I never stained my hands with vile work
although the fever of vice has burned them;
I hobbled my lambs for your sacrifices.

Lord, my poor eyes of impure sight
are lost in the labyrinths of my dark paths,
but when I can, I look toward your heights.

Lord, in vain I purify my exhausted ears
by listening to your voice's song. My ears
hear only howling, howling and howling.

LA GRAN PLEGARIA

El tiempo es hambre y el espacio es frío
orad, orad, que sólo la plegaria
puede saciar las ansias del vacío.

El sueño es una roca solitaria
en donde el águila del alma anida:
soñad, soñad, entre la vida diaria.

THE GREAT PRAYER*

Time is hunger, space is cold.
Pray, pray, for only prayer
can quiet the anguish of the void.

Dream is a solitary rock
where the eagle of the soul nests.
Dream, dream away your everyday live.

---

* inscribed on the poet's tomb in the cathedral of León, Nicaragua

Salomón de la Selva

(1893-1958)

De la Selva was one of the first politically active poets of his country. Much of this activist work was realized in the United States. At the age of twenty-three, the poet was teaching Spanish and French, organizing poetry groups and giving controversial lectures at Williams College in Massachusetts. He moved among the elite literary circles of the epoch and was a very close friend of Edna St. Vincent Millay (her poem, "Recuerdo" is about one of their excursions together). De la Selva even published his first book, *Tropical Town and Other Poems,* in English in 1918. Through-out his life, the poet was involved in politics on a high level. He was personal secretary to the pioneer labor leader, Samuel Gompers. He also worked with Henry Wallace, Vice President under Franklin Roosevelt. In 1930, de la Selva directed a strong campaign in favor of Sandino and the war against U.S. troops occupying Nicaragua. The poet was also the first Hispanic American to be nominated for the Nobel Prize. De la Selva's actions are significant in that they signal the first attempt on the part of Nicaraguan intellectuals to reverse the flow of culture from the United States by working outside Nicaragua.

TROPICAL TOWN*

Blue, pink and yellow houses, and, afar,
The cemetery, where the green trees are.

Sometimes you see a hungry dog pass by,
And there are always buzzards in the sky.
Sometimes you hear the big cathedral bell,
A blindman rings it; and sometimes you hear
A rumbling ox-cart that brings wood to sell.
Else nothing ever breaks the ancient spell
That holds the town asleep, save, once a year,
The Easter festival...

                    I come from there,
And when I tire of hoping, and despair
Is heavy over me, my thoughts go far,
Beyond that length of lazy street, to where
The lonely green trees and the white graves are.

---

* Written originally in English.

LA BALA

La bala que me hiera
será bala con alma.

El alma de esa bala
será como sería
la canción de una rosa
si las flores cantaran,
o el olor de un topacio
si las piedras olieran,
o la piel de una música
si nos fuese posible
tocar a las canciones
desnudas con las manos.

Si me hiere el cerebro
me dirá: Yo buscaba
sondear tu pensamiento.
Y si me hiere el pecho
me dirá: Yo quería
decirte ¡que te quiero!

THE BULLET

The bullet that wounds me
will be a bullet with a soul.

The soul of that bullet
will be as the song
of a rose would be
if flowers could sing,
or the smell of topaz
if stones gave off an odor,
or the skin of music
if it were possible
to touch the naked
songs with our hands.

If it wounds my brain
it will tell me: I was only
probing your thoughts.
And if it wounds my chest
it will say: I wanted
to tell you, I love you!

de SERMÓN DEL PADRE DAMIEN

Molokai, SEGUNDO DOMINGO DE JUNIO, 1885

Nosotros los leprosos
alabemos a Dios. Sólo El es santo.
Celebremos a Dios con alegría
porque hay seres alegres.
Celebremos las flores,
los finos tallos, los lustrados pétalos.
Celebremos las hojas de los árboles,
las ramas y los troncos, y el meneo
de la arboleda cuando le da el viento.
Celebremos el revolotear de las abejas
y de las mariposas,
atareadas más bien que juguetonas.
Celebremos el canto
de los pequeños pájaros que cantan
y el graznido
de las aves que sólo graznar saben
y hacen reír graznando.

Celebremos el mar de hermosas olas
y de brillantes islas.
Relucientes las playas todo el día,
después de que anochece
es dulce echarse en ellas tibias.
Y a todas horas es alegre el convite
de los ruidosos tumbos encrespados
y el ir en las piraguas mar adentro
y de isla en isla, cantando contra el viento
que sabe a sal y nos empuja al canto
a la garganta abierta.

. . . .

from THE SERMON OF FATHER DAMIEN

Molokai, SECOND SUNDAY OF JUNE, 1885

We, the lepers,
praise God. He alone is holy.
Let us happily rejoice in God
for life itself is joyous.
Let us rejoice in the flowers
with their thin stems and shining petals.
Let us rejoice in the leaves
and the branches and the trunks of trees
when they sway in the wind.
Let us rejoice in the way
bees and butterflies move
as they work rather than play.
Let us rejoice in the song
of the small birds that sing
and in the cawing
of the birds that know only how to caw
and make us laugh with their cawing.

Let us rejoice in the sea's lovely waves
and brilliant islands.
The beaches sparkle all day long
and after dusk
it is sweet to lie down on the warm sand
and hear at all hours the call
of the rumbling breakers
while someone paddles out to sea in a canoe
and goes from island to island. And it makes us
sing with our throats open wide
to the wind that tastes like salt.

.   .   .   .

Celebremos el llamear de las velas
y las sombras que se recortan sobre las claras paredes
y el salir a las puertas para decir los adioses
y echarles un vistazo a la luna y las estrellas
y tomar una fresca bocanada del aire
oloroso a las flores olorosas de noche,
y luego el acostarse
en las mullidas camas, entre limpias
sábanas más frescas que el cuerpo,
y el darse al sueño confianzudamente
sin el temor de la traición de la muerte
que tan lenta nos llega a los leprosos.

Celebremos
en el inquieto lunes y toda la semana
el ir los hombres al trabajo
y el buen sudor que refresca
y el encogerse y estirarse los músculos
al hacer fuerzas,
y el hacerse duros los hermosos callos en las manos
y el buen cansancio.

. . . .

Nosotros los leprosos
celebremos lo limpio.
Todo lo limpio es santo.
Todo lo lleno de salud es santo.
Todo lo suave y oloroso es santo.
Es reflejo de Dios, voz de Dios y mensaje
y promesa de Dios, para nosotros
los leprosos, hermanos.

Let us rejoice in the flickering of candles
and in the shadows they cast on the light walls
when we go to our doorways to say goodbye
and we look at the moon and stars
and take a deep breath of fresh air
and smell the flowers that bloom at night,
and then lie down
on soft beds between clean sheets
cooler than our bodies
and fall asleep boldly
without the fear of the treachery of death
which comes so slowly to lepers like us.

Let us rejoice
on restless Monday and all week long
while we work
and the sweat refreshes us
and our muscles expand and contract
as they toil.
The beautiful callouses harden on our hands
and we feel good because we are tired.

. . . .

We, the lepers,
praise what is clean.
All that is clean is holy.
All that is full of health is holy.
All that is soft and fragrant is holy.
It is the reflection of God, the voice of God,
the message and promise of God, for us —
lepers, brothers.

José Coronel Urtecho

(1906-   )

In 1927, José Coronel returned to Granada, Nicaragua, from San Francisco, California, where he had been studying the current trends in North American literature. In 1931, a group of poets known as the *Vanguardia,* whose principal members included José Coronel, Luis Alberto Cabrales, Pablo Antonio Cuadra, Joaquin Pasos, Manolo Cuadra and Alberto Ordoñez, began to publish their poems and manifestos. Coronel, the iconoclast, had launched the revolution with his wonderfully disrespectful *"Oda a Rubén Darío".* According to Ernesto Cardenal, "the fight was not against Darío, but against Darío's falsifiers." The *vanguardistas* viewed their own poetry as "Anti-Academic and Anti-Parnassus in order to fight against the rhetorical literature that inundated the country." This new poetry utilized conversational language, collage, free verse, dialogue, humor and innovative linguistic music from traditional and popular sources. The only permanent factor in Coronel's own poetry is the insatiable desire for experimentation. He has also written essays on the history of his country as well as its cuisine and has comprehensively translated North American poetry. José Coronel, a great teacher who has indelibly influenced generations of Nicaraguan writers with his criticism, praise and lucidity, continues to write from his farm on the *Río Medio Queso.*

RETRATO DE LA MUJER DE TU PRÓJIMO

Fuge litora Circe
Ovidio

Cuando yo los pronuncio, tus ojos lloran
—Minna es tu nombre y cabe en tu sonrisa—
Yo por tí cedo y casi con sentido.

¿Oyes esa mirada que entre tus rizos trina?
Yo estoy más hondo, pero tú estás fuera.
Tuya es la forma y la piel de la poma.

No porque ceda tengo menos sueño.
Nada es lo espeso o ves al ciervo que huye.
Tú te escribes con lápiz —pero cerca—

Cárcel es esto, si no fuera lecho
de leche y sal, porque río lo siento.
Sácame con el ojo, mírame con el dedo.

Vamos por partes:
Dije que el mármol.
El pelo era la hierba el pie descalzo

el pie era mucho donde estaba el ciervo
el pie de fuego el pelo estiércol.
Todo esto fuera pero de veneno...

Ahora
      (suena el teléfono)
Ahora
      (ya estoy despierto)
Ahora
      (Me levanto, me baño, me afeito, me visto, me bebo un
jugo de naranja y bajo al comedor del hotel, donde nos
encontramos y cambiamos saludos; tomo "La Estrella",
pero atisbo todos tus movimientos. Tú te sientas a la mesa y
yo me hallo completamente despierto, no se me escapa el
movimiento sin sentido de las cosas, pero lo voy atando todo
en la tela convencional de las preposiciones, las conjun-
ciones y los verbos, de tal manera que sin dificultad hago un
soneto como los que hago cuando estoy despierto sobre la
superficie de la tierra.

PORTRAIT OF THY NEIGHBOR'S WIFE

Fuge litora Circe
Ovid

When I pronounce them, your eyes cry
—Minna is your name and it fits in your smile—
I yield to you and it almost makes sense.

Do you hear that look that trills among your curls?
I am deeper here, but you are away.
Yours is the form and the skin of the apple.

Not because it yields am I less sleepy.
Nothing is thickness or you see the fleeing deer.
You are written in pencil—but nearby—

This is jail, if it were not a bed
made of milk and salt because to me it feels like river.
Pluck me out with your eye, watch me with your finger.

Let us go part by part:
I said that marble.
The hair was the grass the foot bare

the foot was too much where the deer was
the foot of fire the hair dung.
All this outside but poisonous...

Now
    (the telephone rings)
Now
    (I am awake)
Now
    (I get up, take a shower, shave, get dressed, drink some orange juice,
and go down to the dining room in the hotel, where we meet and greet
each other; I buy "La Estrella" but glimpse your every move. You sit
down at the table and I find myself completely awake, the senseless
movement of things does not escape me, but I tie it all up in the
conventional web of prepositions, conjunctions and verbs, in such a
manner that without much difficulty I write a sonnet like those I write
when I am awake on the surface of the earth.

Copio el soneto:

Te sientas a la mesa, sola y miras
las cinco rosas rojas del florero;
las arreglas mejor, con pulcro esmero,
y dulcemente su perfume aspiras.

Ya vas a suspirar, mas no suspiras.
Mueves con sólo un dedo el cenicero,
y acercándolo a tí, lees el letrero
que dice: "Made in U.S.A.", y lo retiras.

Por un instante, permaneces quieta,
y al ir a desdoblar la servilleta,
cortas, de pronto, el gesto comenzado

pues ves el timbre y lo suenas de prisa;
mientras se abre en tu boca una sonrisa
que se deshace cuando acude el criado.

Así podría es claro, continuar una infinita secuencia de
sonetos, anotando tus movimientos hasta donde "La
Estrella" no es lo mismo porque el peligro en que se
encuentra la mujer que mató a su marido no pasa de un
desfile en la ciudad donde los precios suben mientras los
japoneses tienen listos suficientes hombres, pero gira y se ve
claro el punto negro, o bien dorado, allí donde está aquello
que nos impide como si fuera inconfesable y vamos con
tantos generales en el aire negro cuando leíamos a Lan-
celoto y el aire estaba lleno de mujeres —the air was full of
women...)

El pie era el sol.
Hagamos un esfuerzo:
Demos cifras exactas.
Datos concretos.

Supongamos
que estamos despiertos.
Era a la izquierda masa
de rosa pero cemento.

I copy the sonnet:

You sit at the table, alone in the room
watching five red roses in the vase there,
arranging them better with tidy care,
and sweetly inhaling all their perfume.

You are going to sigh, but you do not sigh.
With just one finger you move the ashtray.
You see that it says, when you have it nearby,
"Made in U.S.A.". You push it away.

You remain still for an instant only.
You take the napkin as if you are going
to unfold it, but then you stop, suddenly.

You see the bell which you hurriedly ring;
while on your mouth you feel a smile open
that undoes itself when the servant comes in.

It is clear that I could go on like this with an infinite sequence of sonnets, annotating your movements until "La Estrella" is not the same because the danger which afflicts the woman who killed her husband does not pass in the city's parade where the prices rise while the Japanese have sufficient men ready, but spins and one clearly sees the black or golden point; that which impedes us as if it were not confessable is over there and we go with so many generals in the black air when we were reading to Lancelot and *the air was full of women...*)

The foot was the sun.
Let us make an effort:
Let us give exact amounts.
Concrete data.

Let us suppose
that we are awake.
It was to the left mass
of rose but cement.

Muro de pie si pie de muro.
Muro infranqueable si pie oscuro
de aurora y nube a luz en masa
forma otra vez que fruta grita.

Pero era música.

Como escalera
estaba abierta.

¿Oyes los ojos de tus dos pasos?
Están abiertos.
Súbense temblando
donde muge el pelo.

¿Qué es lo más agrio?
Risa contra el viento.
De harina de flores
a flores de estiércol.

Lo rojo y lo negro
(Le rouge et le noir)
Si pardo oro siento.
Si lo bebo viento.

Pie si pelo a falo
del pelo descalzo.
De veneno a polen
no de canto a llanto.

Tú estás afuera:

Porque tu frío es río como tibio
lecho de río a pelo y contrapelo —
raudal de mano y brisa de colochos.

Queda en la superficie de los ojos
lo que también de piel a nieve sucia
sin ver la sangre no confiesa angustia.

Wall of foot if foot of wall.
Unfreeable wall if dark foot
from dawn and cloud to light en masse,
form again that fruit shouts.

But it was music.

It was as open
as a stairway.

Do you hear the eyes of your two steps?
They are open.
They go up trembling
to where the hair bellows.

What is most bitter?
Laughter against the wind.
From flour of flowers
to flowers of dung.

The red and the black
(Le rouge et le noir)
If I feel drab, gold.
If I drink it, wind.

Foot if hair to phallus
of hair barefoot.
From poison to pollen
not from song to scream.

You are outside:

Because your coldness is river like tepid riverbed
going with the grain and against the grain
torrent of hand and breeze of woodshavings.

What remains on the surface of the eyes
that which also from skin to dirty snow
without seeing the blood confesses no anguish.

Allí donde se apuesta a quién es bella
tu cara corre como piedra pómez
nadie se apunta sino de tus pechos:

¿Quién te recuerda como palmavera?
Sólo que el aire se abre a tu velamen.
Más que de vela espeso para beso.

Pero es el ojo y mucho es ya beberlo
ya no hay descanso ni en tu piel de arena
porque respiras y tus alas vuelan.

¿Qué va de ciervo a zarpa de pantera?
Quedo de miedo hocico de gacela
de la ventana a la nariz no hay tregua.

Tú ya has olido la acritud del polen
que no es de leche el tumbo de la yegua
ni rompe el aire el trigo como el niño.

Aquí te desdibujo donde el color revienta
son otras lenguas que los pulsos trenzan
la boca avanza y ya no se detiene.

Rompiendo cercas corre como de hombre
brama en la mar la sal como de yegua
pero es espuma roja ostenta-pétalos.

No te parezca aroma que respiras
de suspiros que brisa o que sonrisa
que resoplido a mar fronda de espuma.

Ya es mitológico el que sopla acceso
de espuma en risco rota envuelve a Circe
ni Ulises sabio cerdos bajo el lecho.

No tocaré tus manos con recuerdos
ya de tus pechos no soporto el viento
busco descanso fuera de tu sueño.

There where one wagers on who is beautiful
your face runs like pumice
no one bets except from your breasts:

Who remembers you as springpalm?
Only the wind shall open itself to all your sails.
More than sail thick to kiss.

But to drink the eye is already too much.
There is no longer rest on your skin of sand
because you breathe and your wings fly.

What goes from deer to panther's paw?
I am quiet with fear snout of gazelle
from the window to the nose there is no truce.

You have already smelled the acridity of pollen
that is not of milk the falling wave of the mare
nor breaks the air the wheat like the child.

Here I unsketch you where color explodes
the pulses plait other tongues
the mouth advances and no longer stops.

Breaking fences it runs like a man
the salt in the ocean whinnies like a mare
but it is the red surf petal-displayer.

You shall not seem the aroma you breathe
of sighs that smiles or that breeze
that snorting to sea fronds of surf.

Now mythological what blows access
of broken surf on crag envelops Circe
nor wise Ulysses pigs beneath the bed.

I will not touch your hands with remembrance
from your breasts I cannot bear the wind
I search for rest outside your sleep.

Sueño que no es tormenta no es oscuro
la realidad pequeña como templo
de casa y barco ancla del cambio.

Nombre de regla libra lo que el vórtice
metro y balanza que de santo credo
no de demonio — mar de agua bendita.

Quedan palabras rojas como boyas
que a cada lado son el santo y seña
somos de abismos entre cuatro sueños.

La cadena y la cruz sellan tu pecho
descalza como monja pie de cuero
si busco el faro y si lo gano pierdo:

Gana el gusano
la batalla de la mano.

Dream that is not storm is not obscure
the small reality like the temple
of house and ship anchor of change.

Name of measure frees what the vortex
meter and balance that from sacred creed
not from demon—sea of holy water.

The words remain red like buoys
that to each side are passwords
we of abyss between four dreams.

The chain and the cross seal your chest
barefoot as a nun leather foot
if I look for the lighthouse and I reach it I lose:

The worm wins
the battle of the hand.

Pablo Antonio Cuadra

(1912-   )

Pablo Antonio Cuadra has lived through the series of catastrophes, from the occupation by the U.S. Marines in the 1920's and 1930's to the final years of terror under Somoza, that comprises a major part of Nicaraguan history. In the search for a poetry capable of uniting the fragmented reality of Nicaragua, Cuadra returns to a past cultural identity, unearths it as if it were an archeological object, and makes it come to life in his poems. Since history is usually told by the conquerors and not by the vanquished, Cuadra's poetry recovers the history of the indigenous people of Nicaragua who have been erased in time by their oppressors. The combination in Cuadra's work of Greco-Roman and *nahuatl* mythology along with the poet's fierce nationalism and Christian compassion led Ernesto Cardenal to proclaim Cuadra "the most Nicaraguan of all our poets". As Director of *La Prensa,* Cuadra spearheaded the intellectual opposition to the Somoza regime.

EL BARCO NEGRO

Cifar, entre su sueño oyó los gritos
y el ululante caracol en la neblina
del alba. Miró el barco
   —inmóvil—
   fijo entre las olas.

   —Si oyes
   en la oscura
   mitad de la noche
   —en aguas altas—
   gritos que preguntan
   por el puerto:
      dobla el timón
        y huye

Recortado en la espuma
el casco oscuro y carcomido,
(—¡Marinero!, gritaban—)
las jarcias rotas
meciéndose y las velas
negras y podridas
        (—¡Marinero!—)
Puesto de pie, Cifar, abrazó el mástil

   —Si la luna
   ilumina sus rostros
   cenizos y barbudos
   Si te dicen
   —Marinero ¿dónde vamos?
   Si te imploran:
   —¡Marinero, enséñanos
   el puerto!
   dobla el timón
   y huye!

Hace tiempo zarparon
Hace siglos navegan en el sueño

   Son tus propias preguntas
   perdidas en el tiempo.

THE BLACK SHIP

Cifar, in his dream, heard the cries
and the howling conch in the fog
at dawn. He watched the ship
    —immobile—
fixed between waves.

    —If you hear
    in the dark
    midnight
    —in high waters—
    cries that ask
    for the port:
        turn the rudder
            and flee

The dark hull, gnawed away,
outlined in the surf,
(—Sailor!, they cried—)
the broken rigging
rocking and the sails
black and rotten
            (—Sailor!—)
Standing up, Cifar embraced the mast

    If the moon
    illuminates their faces
    ashen and bearded
    If they ask you
    —Sailor, where are we bound?
    If they implore you:
    —Sailor, show us the way
    to the port!
    turn the rudder
    and flee!

They set sail a long time ago
They navigated in the dream centuries ago

    They are your own questions
    lost in time.

EL CABALLO AHOGADO

Después de la borrasca
en el oscuro silencio
miraron sobre las aguas
flotando
el caballo muerto.

—Es la crecida, dijeron
los pescadores
　　　　　y detuvieron
　　　　　la barca.
Las olas
movían sus largas crines.
El ojo, abierto,
fijo su asombro
en el cielo.
　　　　Tendido, la muerte
　　　　lo hacía inmenso.

Sintieron
como un extraño
presagio

　　y vieron
una corona
de gaviotas blancas
en el viento.

THE DROWNED HORSE

After the tempest
in the dark silence
they watched the dead horse
floating
upon the waters.

—It's the floods, said
the fishermen
                and they stopped
                their boat.
The waves
moved its long mane.
The eye, open,
fixed its fright
on the sky.
            Stretched out, death
            had made it immense.

They sensed
a strange
omen
            and saw
    a crown
    of white gulls
    in the wind.

LA LANCHA DE EL PIRATA

En lo más oscuro
de la noche
haciendo ruta
de San Carlos
a Granada
   escuchamos cantos
   gritos
      y guitarras.
Al acercarnos
conocieron la vela
—¡Cifar! ¡Tirá la espía!
Tenemos guaro y mujeres!
...Bailaban
     —y sonaban
a golpe de talón
como un tambor
la inmóvil lancha—
pero otros en la borda
desesperados imploraban:
—¡Cifar! ¡llevanos a Granada!
¡te pagamos, Cifar!
¡tu boca es la medida!

   Eran vivanderas,
   angustiados pasajeros
   comerciantes de los puertos
   anclados en la noche
   y obligados
   a la juerga y al desvelo.

   Compasivo Cifar, tiró la espía
   y abordó la lancha de Corea
   —¡Cristóbal! ¡loco
   irresponsable!
      gritó entre risas
      mientras ayudaba
      a saltar al barco
      a los tristes viajeros.

THE PIRATE'S BOAT

In the darkest
of the night
en route
from San Carlos
to Granada
          we heard songs
          shouts
                    and guitars.
Getting closer
they recognized our sail
"Cifar! Drop anchor!
We've got booze and women!"
... They were dancing
                    — the stamping
heels against
the immobile boat
like a drum —
but others on board
desperately implored:
"Cifar, take us to Granada!
We'll pay you, Cifar!
Let your mouth be the measure!"

          They were sutlers
          anguished passengers
          merchants of port
          anchored in the night
          and obliged
          to stay awake for the binge.

Compassionate Cifar dropped anchor
and boarded the boat from Korea.
"Cristóbal! Crazy
good for nothing!"
                    he shouted amidst laughter
                    as he helped
                    the sad travelers
                    leap to the ship.

Las guitarras
arreciaron la lluvia de sus sones.
—¡Cifar! gritaban
—¡Cifar! dónde está el hombre?!
y manos obsequiosas
le rodeaban de botellas.
      —¡Sólo un trago
      y nos vamos! dijo con honda
      convicción Cifar.

Pero oyó entonces
una voz que lo llamaba
y vio la loca cabellera
suelta
      de Mirna
bailando
entre el enjambre de estrellas.

…Menos mal que el Lago
estaba quieto.
Menos mal que las estrellas
                    son
                    len-
                    tas
para contar el tiempo…

                The guitars
made the rain of their sound grow louder.
"Cifar!" they shouted.
"Cifar! Where is he?"
and obsequious hands
surrounded him with bottles.
                        "One drink and we'll
                        be on our way," said Cifar
                        with deep conviction.

But then he heard
a voice calling him
and saw the crazy
loose hair
            of Mirna
dancing
among the swarming stars.

. . . Luckily the Lake
was quiet.
Luckily the stars
                        are
                        slow
at telling time . . .

CANCIÓN PARA UNAS MUCHACHAS

Esas muchachas que se creen solas
danzan desnudas en la chispeante arena
al ritmo de las olas.

Qué haré cuando otra vez las mire,
cuando en la noche llegue y quietas
contemple su timidez, sentadas
a la luz de la lumbre y mi oscuro
y terco corazón, saltando como un perro,
muerda el recuerdo de sus cuerpos desnudos?

SONG FOR SOME GIRLS

Those girls who think they are alone
dance naked on the sparkling sand
to the rhythm of the waves.

What will I do when I see them again,
when I arrive tonight and contemplate
their shyness as they sit quietly
in firelight and my dark and stubborn
heart, leaping like a dog,
bites the memory of their naked bodies?

LA NOCHE ES UNA MUJER DESCONOCIDA

Preguntó la muchacha al forastero:
—¿Por qué no pasas? En mi hogar
está encendido el fuego.

Contestó el peregrino: —Soy poeta,
sólo deseo conocer la noche.

Ella, entonces, echó cenizas sobre el fuego
y aproximó en la sombra su voz al forastero:
—¡Tócame! —dijo—. ¡Conocerás la noche!

THE NIGHT IS AN UNKNOWN WOMAN

The girl asked the stranger,
"Why don't you come in?
The fire is lit at my place."

The wanderer answered, "I'm a poet,
I only want to know the night."

Then she threw ashes on the fire
and her voice in the shadow drew near the stranger.
"Touch me," she said. "You'll know the night!"

ESCRITO EN UNA PIEDRA DEL CAMINO
CUANDO LA PRIMERA ERUPCIÓN

¡Lloraremos sobre las huellas de los que huyen de
    Acahualinca!
Aquí comenzó nuestro éxodo.

Oyeron la gran voz cavernosa del monstruo.
Desde los altos árboles miraron el sucio gigante decapitado,
la espalda rugosa, solamente el rugoso pecho vomitando ira.

Abandonaremos nuestra Patria y nuestra parentela
porque ha dominado nuestra tierra un dios estéril.

Nuestro pueblo miró el gigante sin mente,
oyó el bramido de la fuerza sin rostro.

¡No viviremos bajo el dominio de la ciega potencia!
¡Quebraremos nuestras piedras de moler,
                nuestras tinajas,
                nuestros comales,
para aligerar el paso de los exilados!

Allí quedaron nuestras huellas,
                sobre la ceniza.

WRITTEN ON A ROADSIDE STONE
DURING THE FIRST ERUPTION

We will cry over the footprints of those who fled from Acahualinc
Our exodus began here.

They heard the cavernous voice of the monster.
From the high trees they watched the dirty decapitated giant,
the rugged back, only the rugged breast vomiting anger.

We will abandon our country and our kin
because a sterile god has dominated our land.

Our people watched the mindless giant,
they heard the roar of the faceless force.

We will not live under the blind power's domination!
We will break our grinding stones,
                    our earthen jugs,
                    the plates we cook on,
to lighten the load of the exiled!

Here, our footprints remained
                    upon the ash.

POR LOS CAMINOS VAN LOS CAMPESINOS...

De dos en dos,
de diez en diez,
de cien en cien,
de mil en mil,
descalzos van los campesinos
con la chamarra y el fusil.

De dos en dos los hijos han partido,
de cien en cien las madres han llorado,
de mil en mil los hombres han caído,
y hecho polvo ha quedado
su sueño en la chamarra, su vida en el fusil.

El rancho abandonado,
la milpa sola, el frijolar quemado.
El pájaro volando
sobre la espiga muda
y el corazón llorando
su lágrima desnuda.

De dos en dos,
de diez en diez,
de cien en cien,
de mil en mil,
descalzos van los campesinos
con la chamarra y el fusil.

De dos en dos,
de diez en diez,
de cien en cien,
de mil en mil,
¡por los caminos van los campesinos
a la guerra civil!

THE CAMPESINOS GO DOWN THE ROADS

Two by two,
ten by ten,
by hundreds
and thousands,
the *campesinos* go barefoot
with their bedrolls and their rifles.

Two by two the sons have left,
hundreds of mothers have cried,
thousands of men have fallen
and turned to dust forever
dreaming on their bedrolls
about the life that was their rifle.

The abandoned ranch,
the lonely fields of corn,
the fields of beans destroyed by fire.
The birds flying over mute stalks
and the heart crying
its naked tears.

Two by two,
ten by ten,
by hundreds and thousands
the *campesinos* are leaving
barefoot with their bedrolls and their rifles.

Two by two,
ten by ten,
by hundreds
and thousands
the *campesinos* go down the roads
to fight the civil war!

INTERIORIDAD DE DOS ESTRELLAS QUE ARDEN

a Mario Cajina-Vega

Al que combatió por la Libertad
se le dio una estrella, vecina
a la luminosa madre muerta al alumbrar.
—¿Fue grande tu dolor? —preguntó
el Guerrero

        —No tanto como el gozo
de dar un nuevo hombre al mundo.
—¿Y tu herida —dijo ella—
fue honda y torturante?
        —No tanto
como el gozo de dar al hombre un mundo nuevo.
—¿Y conociste a tu hijo?
        —¡Nunca!
—¿Y conociste el fruto de tu lucha?
        —Morí antes.
—¿Duermes? —preguntó el Guerrero.
—Sueño —respondió la madre.

AT THE HEART OF TWO BURNING STARS

to Mario Cajina-Vega

He who fought for Liberty
was given a star, neighboring
the luminous mother who died in childbirth.
"How great was your pain?" asked
the Warrior.
                    "Not so great as my joy
in giving a new man to the world," she said.
"And did your deep wound
torture you?"
                    "Not so much
as my joy in giving man a new world."
"And did you know your son?"
                         "Never!"
"And did you know the fruit of your struggle?"
                         "I died too soon."
"Do you sleep?" asked the Warrior.
"I dream," replied the mother.

Joaquin Pasos
(1914-1947)

Joaquin Pasos was the most precocious member of the *Vanguardia*. There is a wide variety of themes and tones in Pasos' work, from the playful satire of *Chinfonía burguesa* (written with José Coronel) to the apocalyptic long poem, *"Canto de guerra de las cosas"*. Pasos never left Nicaragua. But the fantastic voyages he makes to Germany, to Norway, with Captain Cook, etc. in *Poemas de un joven que nunca ha viajado* surge musically like the waves beneath his imaginary boat. Pasos even wrote a series of poems in English. And he was interested in describing the interior world of the indigenous people of his country. In *Misterio indio,* Pasos constructs the interior landscape of the indians and sees the external landscape through their eyes. Pasos wrote his monumental *"Canto de guerra de las cosas"* during the years of World War II. The poem describes a world in which reality and dream have merged on the smoking battlefield of the human psyche. Like Eliot's "The Waste Land", *"Canto de guerra de las cosas"* bears witness to the global destruction of war. It is the poet's legacy to the Nuclear Age. Even though Pasos died prematurely, his works remain among the most important Nicaragua has produced.

LOS INDIOS CIEGOS

Abramos un camino en el aire,
para mirarnos,
busquemos un rincón en el aire
para acostarnos.

Sin luz en el cuerpo
sólo con fuego.
Este color de sombra tiene tu cara.
Este color de sombra es la sombra de tu alma.

Abramos un camino en el aire
con tu brazo.
Si no te ven mis ojos, que te vea
mi carne.

¡Ah! No tenemos luz en el cuerpo.
Tenemos fuego.

THE BLIND INDIANS

Let's open a road in the air
so we can look at each other.
Let's look for a corner in the air
so we can lie down.

Without light in our bodies,
only fire.
Your face has this color of shadow.
This color of shadow, shadow of your soul.

Let's open a road in the air
with your arm.
If my eyes do not see you,
my flesh will.

Ah! We do not have light in our bodies.
We have fire.

TORMENTA

Nuestro viento furioso grita a través de palmas gigantes,
sordos bramidos bajan del cielo incendiados con lenguas de leopardos,
nuestro viento furioso cae de lo alto.

El golpe de su cuerpo sacude las raíces de los grandes árboles,
salen del suelo los escarabajos,
las serpientes machos.

Nuestro viento furioso sigue su camino mojado,
es el jugo oscuro de la tarde que beben los toros salvajes,
es el castigador del campo.

Los hombres oyen en silencio los gemidos del aire
con el alma quebrada, el cuerpo en alto,
los pies y la cara de barro.

Las indias jóvenes salen al patio, rompen sus camisas,
ofrecen al viento sus senos desnudos, que él se encarga de afilar
    como volcanes.

TEMPEST

Our furious wind screams through giant palm trees,
it howls from the sky and burns with leopard tongues,
our furious wind falls from high above.

The blow of its body shakes the roots
of the great trees, the beetles and mansnakes
crawl from the ground.

Our furious wind follows its wet road,
it is the dark juice of the afternoon drunk by the savage bulls,
it is the scourge of the countryside.

Men listen to the moanings of the air in silence
with broken soul, body held high,
mud on feet and face.

The young indian girls go out in the courtyard,
rip open their shirts and offer their naked breasts.
The wind hones them like volcanoes.

CEMENTERIO

La tierra aburrida de los hombres que roncan
es aquella que habitan los pájaros pobres,
las gallinas que comen las piedras
las lechuzas que braman de noche.
Una jaula de arena, una urna de lodo
es la tierra aburrida de los hombres que roncan.
Una jícara negra, una seca tinaja,
un carbón, una mierda, una cáscara.

En la tierra aburrida de los hombres que roncan
donde viven los pájaros tristes, los pájaros sordos,
los cultivos de piedras, los sembrados de escobas.
Protejan los escarabajos, cuiden los sapos
el tesoro de estiércol de los pájaros pobres.
Los pájaros enfermos, los vestidos de sombra,
los que habitan la tierra de los hombres que roncan.

Tengo un triste recuerdo de esa tierra sin horas,
la picada de pájaros, la que se desmorona.
Con murciélagos me persigue de noche
su horizonte de barro y su luna de broza.
En la tierra aburrida de los hombres que roncan
se hizo piedra mi sueño, y después se hizo polvo.

CEMETERY

The boring land of the snoring men
is that place where poor birds live,
where hens eat stones,
owls screech at night.
Cage of sand, urn of mud:
the boring land of the snoring men.
Black gourd bowl, dry jug,
pieces of shit and coal, a rind.

In the boring land of the snoring men
where the sad birds live with the deaf birds,
the cultivations of stones, the plantings of brooms.
The beetles will protect, the frogs will guard
the treasure of the poor birds' dung.
The sick birds, the ones dressed in shadow,
those who inhabit the boring land of the snoring men.

I have a sad memory of that hourless land,
the peck of the birds that crumbles away.
It pursues me at night with bats:
its mud horizon and underbrush moon.
In the boring land of the snoring men
my dream became stone, and then became dust.

LOS INDIOS VIEJOS

Los hombres viejos, muy viejos, están sentados
junto a sus cabras, junto a sus pequeños animales mansos.
Los hombres viejos están sentados junto a un río
que siempre va despacio.
Ante ellos el aire detiene su marcha,
el viento pasa, contemplándolos,
los toca con cuidado
para no desbaratarles sus corazones de ceniza.

Los hombres viejos sacan al campo sus pecados,
éste es su único trabajo.
Los sueltan durante el día, pasan el día olvidando,
y en la tarde salen a lazarlos
para dormir con ellos calentándose.

THE OLD INDIANS

The old men, very old, are sitting
next to their goats, next to their small meek animals.
The old men are sitting next to a river
that always goes slowly.
In front of them the air halts its march,
the wind passes, contemplating them,
it touches them with care,
so it doesn't destroy their hearts of ash.

The old men take their sins to the countryside,
this is their only work.
They free them by day, then spend the day forgetting,
and in the afternoon they go out and lasso them
so they can sleep with them and keep warm.

INTERVENTION TIME*
1 p.m.

This hour sings obscenities
over a fat man's belly on good digestion
and it belches the words.

This is why I throw them in English.

Another quality of this after-glut time
is to be special for roughness.

So, we may spit the druggist's shop of the sun

and say: "What
do you want?" and "Go to hell"
The minutes bite like mosquitoes.

This is an Intervention time.
This is an hour to be said by yankee trumpets
just up there in the Campo de Marte.
O! The houses are groggy under the blows of heaven.
You will never get for your hair a ribbon
or a star from the North American banner!

---

* written originally in English

THINGS TO WELCOME LOVE*

Love will call to you some day of June.
Your lonely garden must be quiet and arranged
as if you were to die in solitude.
You must be dressed in an old pink gown,
a burial robe just like a wedding one,
because Love and Death are so near and so far!

Your lonely garden must be full of bees,
the lilies must be gathered in your arms,
then you will sit and wait under the trees.

O, please, a moment! Something is missing in the place.
Under a tree a table must be set,
a table with more flowers and a book,
a silver bell and a teacup.
Let us hang violins from the highest branches.
Let us forget the moon.
Love will come here riding on a bicycle
as softly as this quiet afternoon.

What more? More flowers, yes, more flowers on the benches,
and a little scholar's smile
to dance with the music lesson of your eyes.
Love will call to you some day of these,
maybe it is coming now. You fix my tie
and we shall sit and wait under the trees.

---

* written originally in English

CANTO DE GUERRA DE LAS COSAS

Fratres: Existimoenim quod non sunt condignae passiones
hujus temporis ad futuram gloriam, quae revelabitur in
nobis. Nam exspectatio creaturae revelationem filiorum
Dei exspectat. Vanitati enim creatura subjecta est non
volens, sed propter eum, qui subjecit eam in spe: quia et
ipsa creatura liberabitur a servitute corruptionis in liber-
tatem gloriae filiorum Dei…Scimus enim quod omnis
creaturae ingemiscit, et parturit usque adhuc.

Paulus ad Rom. VIII: 18-22

Cuando lleguéis a viejos, respetaréis la piedra,
si es que llegáis a viejos,
si es que entonces quedó alguna piedra.
Vuestros hijos amarán al viejo cobre,
al hierro fiel.
Recibiréis a los antiguos metales en el seno de vuestras familias,
trataréis al noble plomo con la decencia que corresponde a su carácter
    dulce;
os reconciliaréis con el zinc dándole un suave nombre;
con el bronce considerándolo como hermano del oro,
porque el oro no fue a la guerra por vosotros,
el oro se quedó, por vosotros, haciendo el papel de niño mimado,
vestido de terciopelo, arropado, protegido por el resentido acero…
Cuando lleguéis a viejos, respetaréis al oro,
si es que llegáis a viejos,
si es que entonces quedó algún oro.

El agua es la única eternidad de la sangre.
Su fuerza, hecha sangre. Su inquietud, hecha sangre.
Su violento anhelo de viento y cielo,
hecho sangre.
Mañana dirán que la sangre se hizo polvo,
mañana estará seca la sangre.
Ni sudor, ni lágrimas, ni orina
podrán llenar el hueco del corazón vacío.
Mañana envidiarán la bomba hidráulica de un inodoro palpitante,
la constancia viva de un grifo,
el grueso líquido.
El río se encargará de los riñones destrozados
y en medio del desierto los huesos en cruz pedirán en vano que
    regrese el agua a los cuerpos de los hombres.

WARSONG OF THE THINGS

> Brothers: I consider that the sufferings of this present time
> are not worth comparing with the glory that is to be
> revealed to us. For the creation waits with eager longing
> for the revealing of the children of God. We know that the
> whole creation has been groaning in travail together until
> now...
>
> Romans VIII:18-22

When you reach old age, you will respect stone,
if indeed you reach old age,
if indeed there is any stone left.
Your children will love old copper,
faithful iron.
You will greet ancient metals in your homes,
you will treat noble lead with grace appropriate to its sweet character;
you will be reconciled with zinc, giving it a soft name;
with bronze, by considering it gold's brother,
because gold did not go to war for you.
Gold stayed, for you, playing the role of a spoiled child,
dressed in velvet, bundled up, protected by resentful steel...
When you reach old age, you will respect gold,
if indeed you reach old age,
if indeed there is any gold left.

Water is the sole eternity of blood.
Its strength, made blood. Its disquiet, made blood.
Its violent longing of wind and sky
made blood.
Tomorrow they will say blood became dust,
tomorrow the blood will be dry.
Neither sweat, nor tears, nor urine
will fill the hollow of the empty heart.
Tomorrow they will envy the hydraulic pump of a throbbing watercloset,
the living proof of a spigot,
the thick liquid.
The river will take charge of the ruined kidneys
and in the middle of the desert the crossed bones
will beg the water to return to the bodies of men in vain.

Dadme un motor más fuerte que un corazón de hombre.
Dadme un cerebro de máquina que pueda ser agujereado sin dolor.
Dadme por fuera un cuerpo de metal y por dentro otro cuerpo de metal
igual al del soldado de plomo que no muere,
que no te pide, Señor, la gracia de no ser humillado por tus obras,
como el soldado de carne blanducha, nuestro débil orgullo,
que por tu día ofrecerá la luz de sus ojos,
que por tu metal admitirá una bala en su pecho,
que por tu agua devolverá su sangre.
Y que quiere ser como un cuchillo, al que no puede herir otro cuchillo.

Esta cal de mi sangre incorporada a mi vida
será la cal de mi tumba incorporada a mi muerte,
porque aquí está el futuro envuelto en papel de estaño,
aquí está la ración humana en forma de pequeños ataúdes,
y la ametralladora sigue ardiendo de deseos
y a través de los siglos sigue fiel el amor del cuchillo a la carne.
Y luego, decid si no ha sido abundante la cosecha de balas,
si los campos no están sembrados de bayonetas,
si no han reventado a su tiempo las granadas...
Decid si hay algún pozo, un hueco, un escondrijo
que no sea un fecundo nido de bombas robustas;
decid si este diluvio de fuego líquido
no es más hermoso y más terrible que el de Noé,
sin que haya un arca de acero que resista
ni un avión que regrese con la rama de olivo!

Vosotros, dominadores del cristal, he ahí vuestros vidrios fundidos.
Vuestras casas de porcelana, vuestros trenes de mica,
vuestras lágrimas envueltas en celofán, vuestros corazones de bakelita,
vuestros risibles y hediondos pies de hule,
todo se funde y corre al llamado de guerra de las cosas,
como se funde y se escapa con rencor el acero que ha sostenido una
     estatua.

Los marineros están un poco excitados. Algo les turba su viaje.
Se asoman a la borda y escudriñan el agua,
se asoman a la torre y escudriñan el aire.
Pero no hay nada.
No hay peces, ni olas, ni estrellas, ni pájaros.
Señor capitán, a dónde vamos?
Lo sabremos más tarde.

Give me a motor stronger than a man's heart,
Give me a robot's brain that can be murdered without pain.
Give me an outer body of metal and an inner body of metal
like the lead soldier's that does not die,
that does not beg you, Lord, for the grace not to be humbled by your
    works,
like the soldier of mere flesh, our feeble pride,
who, for your day, will offer the light of his eyes,
who, for your metal, will take a bullet in his chest,
who, for your water, will return his blood.
And who wants to be like a knife, the kind that cannot wound another
    knife.

The ash of my blood incorporated into my life
will be the ash of my tomb incorporated into my death,
because here is the future wrapped in foil,
here is the human ration in the shape of tiny coffins,
and the machine gun burns with desire
and through the centuries the knife's love stays faithful to the flesh.
And then, tell me if the harvest of bullets has not been plentiful,
if the fields are not sown with bayonets,
if the grenades have not exploded on time...
Tell me if there is some well, a hollow, a place to hide
that is not a fertile nest of robust bombs;
tell me if this deluge of liquid fire
is not more beautiful and more terrible than Noah's,
with an ark reinforced with steel
or a plane to fly back with the olive branch!

You, masters of crystal, here are your smelted windows.
Your porcelain houses, your mica trains,
your tears wrapped in celophane, your sheet-metal hearts,
your laughable and stinking rubber feet —
everything melts and flows to the war cry of the things
the way the steel supporting a statue melts and escapes with malice.

The sailors are a little excited. Something troubles their voyage.
They peer over the gunwale and scrutinize the water.
They peer from the crow's nest and scrutinize the air.
But there is nothing.
No fish, no waves, no stars, no birds.
Captain, where are we bound?
Ask me later.

Cuando hayamos llegado.
Los marineros quieren lanzar el ancla,
los marineros quieren saber qué pasa.
Pero no es nada. Están un poco excitados.
El agua del mar tiene un sabor más amargo,
el viento del mar es demasiado pesado.
Y no camina el barco. Se quedó quieto en medio del viaje.
Los marineros se preguntan ¿que pasa? con las manos,
han perdido el habla.
No pasa nada. Están un poco excitados.
Nunca volverá a pasar nada. Nunca lanzarán el ancla.

No había que buscarla en las cartas del naipe ni en los juegos de la
    cábala.
En todas las cartas estaba, hasta en las de amor y en las de navegar.
Todos los signos llevaban su signo.
Izaba su bandera sin color, fantasma de bandera para ser pintada con
    colores de sangre de fantasma,
bandera que cuando flotaba al viento parecía que flotaba el viento.
Iba y venía, iba en el venir, venía en el yendo, como que si fuera
    viniendo.
Subía, y luego bajaba hasta en medio de la multitud y besaba a cada
    hombre.
Acariciaba cada cosa con sus dedos suaves de sobadora de marfil.
Cuando pasaba un tranvía, ella pasaba en el tranvía
cuando pasaba una locomotora, ella iba sentada en la trompa.
Pasaba ante el vidrio de todas las vitrinas,
sobre el río de todos los puentes,
por el cielo de todas las ventanas.
Era la misma vida que flota ciega en las calles como una niebla
    borracha.
Estaba de pie junto a todas las paredes como un ejército de mendigos,
era un diluvio en el aire.
Era tenaz, y también dulce, como el tiempo.

Con la opaca voz de un destrozado amor sin remedio,
con el hueco de un corazón fugitivo,
con la sombra del cuerpo
con la sombra del alma, apenas sombra de vidrio,
con el espacio vacío de una mano sin dueño,
con los labios heridos
con los párpados sin sueño,
con el pedazo de pecho donde está sembrado el musgo del resentimiento

When we get there.
The sailors want to drop anchor,
the sailors want to know what's going on.
It's nothing. They're just a little excited.
The seawater tastes more bitter,
the wind from the sea is too strong.
And the ship does not move: becalmed in the middle of the voyage.
The sailors ask themselves *what's going on?* with their hands;
they have lost their speech.
It's nothing. They're just a little excited.
Nothing ever again. They will never drop anchor.

It wasn't necessary to look for her in the deck of cards or in games of
divination.
She was in all the cards, even in those of love and navigation.
All signs carried her sign.
She raised her colorless banner, phantom banner to be painted with colors
of phantom's blood
When the banner floated in the wind it seemed as if the wind floated.
She came and went, went in the coming, came in the going, as if she were
coming.
She went up and then came down in the middle of the multitude and kissed
each man.
She caressed each thing with her soft fingers of ivory taffy.
When a trolley car passed, she passed in the trolley car;
when a locomotive passed, she was sitting on the cowcatcher.
She passed — by all the shop windows,
upon the river of all the bridges,
through the sky of all the windows.
She was the same life that floats blindly in the streets like a drunken fog.
She was standing next to all the walls like an army of beggars.
She was a deluge in the air.
She was tenacious and sweet as well, like time.

With the opaque voice of a love unavoidably destroyed,
with the hollow of a fugitive heart,
with the shadow of the body,
with the shadow of the soul, barely shadow of glass,
with the empty space of an ownerless hand,
with wounded lips,
with sleepless eyelids,
with the place in the chest where the moss of resentment grows

y el narciso,
con el hombro izquierdo
con el hombro que carga las flores y el vino,
con las uñas que aún están adentro
y no han salido,
con el porvenir sin premio, con el pasado sin castigo,
con el aliento,
con el silbido,
con el último bocado de tiempo, con el último sorbo de líquido
con el último verso del último libro.
Y con lo que será ajeno. Y con lo que fue mío.

Somos la orquídea del acero,
florecimos en la trinchera como el moho sobre el filo de la espada,
somos una vegetación de sangre,
somos flores de carne que chorrean sangre,
somos la muerte recién podada
que florecerá muertes y más muertes hasta hacer un inmenso jardín de
    muertes.

Como la enredadera púrpura de filosa raíz,
que corta el corazón y se siembra en la fangosa sangre
y sube y baja según su peligrosa marea.
Así hemos inundado el pecho de los vivos,
somos la selva que avanza.

Somos la tierra presente. Vegetal y podrida.
Pantano corrompido que burbujea mariposas y arco-iris.
Donde tu cáscara se levanta están nuestros huesos llorosos,
nuestro dolor brillante en carne viva,
oh santa y hedionda tierra nuestra,
humus humanus.

Desde mi gris sube mi ávida mirada,
mi ojo viejo y tardo, ya encanecido,
desde el fondo de un vértigo lamoso
sin negro y sin color completamente ciego.
Asciendo como topo hacia un aire
que huele mi vista,
el ojo de mi olfato, y el murciélago
todo hecho de sonido.

and the narcissus,
with the left shoulder,
with the shoulder burdened with flowers and wine,
with the fingernails that are still within
and have not come out,
with the future without reward, with the past without punishment,
with the breath,
with the whistle,
with the last morsel of time, with the last sip of liquid,
with the last line of the last book.
And with that which will be someone else's. And with that which was
    mine.

We are the orchid of the steel,
we flower in the trench like the mold on the edge of the sword,
we are a vegetation of blood,
we are cut-flowers of flesh that spurt blood,
we are the death just pruned
that will bloom death and more deaths until an immense garden of deaths is made

Like the climbing purple vine's sharp root
that cuts the heart and grows in miry blood
and rises and falls according to its dangerous tide.
This is how we have flooded the chest of the living,
we are the advancing jungle.

We are the present earth. Plant-like and rotting.
Corrupt swamp that bubbles butterflies and rainbows.
There, where your shell rises, are our weeping bones,
our brilliant pain in living flesh,
oh, holy and stinking mother earth,
humus humanus.

My eager gaze rises from my grayness,
my old and slow eye, already graying,
from the bottom of a silty dizziness
without black and colorless, completely blind.
I ascend like a mole toward an air
that smells my vision,
the eye of my sense of smell, and the bat
made entirely of sound.

Aquí la piedra es piedra, pero ni el tacto sordo
puede imaginar si vamos o venimos,
pero venimos, sí, desde mi fondo espeso,
pero vamos, ya lo sentimos, en los dedos podridos
y en esta cruel mudez que quiere cantar.

Como un súbito amanecer que la sangre dibuja
irrumpe el violento deseo de sufrir,
y luego el llanto fluyendo como la uña de la carne
y el rabioso corazón ladrando en la puerta.
Y en la puerta un cubo que se palpa
y un camino verde bajo los pies hasta el pozo,
hasta más hondo aún, hasta el agua,
y en el agua una palabra samaritana
hasta más hondo aún, hasta el beso.

Del mar opaco que me empuja
llevo en mi sangre el hueco de su ola,
el hueco de su huida,
un precipicio de sal aposentada.
Si algo traigo para decir, dispensadme,
en el bello camino lo he olvidado.
Por un descuido me comí la espuma,
perdonadme, que vengo enamorado.

Detrás de ti quedan ahora cosas despreocupadas, dulces.
Pájaros muertos, árboles sin riego.
Una hiedra marchita. Un olor de recuerdo.
No hay nada exacto, no hay nada malo ni bueno,
y parece que la vida se ha marchado hacia el país del trueno.
Tú, que viste en un jarrón de flores el golpe de esta fuerza,
tú, la invitada al viento en fiesta,
tú, la dueña de una cotorra y un coche de ágiles ruedas,
tú que miraste a un caballo del tiovivo saltar sobre la verja
y quedar sobre la grama como esperando que lo montasen los niños de la
    escuela,
asiste ahora, con ojos pálidos, a esta naturaleza muerta.

Los frutos no maduran en este aire dormido
sino lentamente, de tal suerte que parecen marchitos,
y hasta los insectos se equivocan en esta primavera sonámbula sin sentido.

Here the stone is stone, but not even the deaf sense of touch
can imagine if we are going or coming,
but we are coming, yes, from my thick depth;
but we are going, already we feel it, in the rotten fingers
and in this cruel muteness that wishes to sing.

Like a sudden dawning that the blood draws,
the violent desire to suffer bursts open,
and then the scream flowing like the fingernail of the flesh
and the rabid heart barking in the doorway.
And in the doorway someone gropes for a bucket,
and a green road beneath the feet down to a well,
down deeper still, down to the water,
and in the water a samaritan word,
down deeper still, down to the kiss.

From the opaque sea that pushes me,
I carry in my blood the hollow of its wave,
the hollow of its fleeing,
a precipice of chambered salt.
If I bring something to say, excuse me;
the beautiful road has made me forget.
I drank the surf through carelessness.
Forgive me. I'm in love.

Behind you now, sweet, unworried things remain.
Dead birds, unwatered trees.
Withered ivy. An odor of remembrance.
There is nothing exact, there is nothing bad nor good,
and it seems that life has left for the country of thunder.
You, who saw in a vase of flowers the blow of this force,
you, guest to the partying wind,
you, master of a parrot and a carriage of agile wheels,
you, who watched a merry-go-round horse leap over the iron gate
and remain on the grass as if waiting for the schoolchildren to mount it,
participate now, with pallid eyes, in this still life.

The fruit ripen in this sleeping air,
but slowly, and with such luck they seem withered,
and even the insects make mistakes in this senseless, somnambulant Spring.

La naturaleza tiene ausente a su marido.
No tienen ni fuerzas suficientes para morir las semillas del cultivo
y su muerte se oye como el hilito de sangre que sale de la boca del hombre
        herido.
Rosas solteronas, flores que parecen usadas en la fiesta del olvido,
débil olor de tumbas, de hierbas que mueren sobre mármoles inscritos.
Ni un solo grito, Ni siquiera la voz de un pájaro o de un niño
o el ruido de un bravo asesino con su cuchillo.
¡Qué dieras hoy por tener manchado de sangre el vestido!
¡Qué dieras por encontrar habitado algún nido!
¡Qué dieras porque sembraran en tu carne un hijo!

Por fin, Señor de los Ejércitos, he aquí el dolor supremo.
He aquí, sin lástimas, sin subterfugios, sin versos,
el dolor verdadero.
Por fin, Señor, he aquí frente a nosotros el dolor parado en seco.
No es un dolor por los heridos ni por los muertos,
ni por la sangre derramada ni por la tierra llena de lamentos
ni por las ciudades vacías de casas ni por los campos llenos de huérfanos.
Es el dolor entero.
No pueden haber lágrimas ni duelo
ni palabras ni recuerdos,
pues nada cabe ya dentro del pecho.
Todos los ruidos del mundo forman un gran silencio.
Todos los hombres del mundo forman un solo espectro.
En medio de este dolor, ¡soldado!, queda tu puesto
vacío o lleno.
Las vidas de los que quedan están con huecos,
tienen vacíos completos,
como si se hubieran sacado bocados de carne de sus cuerpos.
Asómate a este boquete, a éste que tengo en el pecho,
para ver cielos e infiernos.
Mira mi cabeza hendida por millares de agujeros:
a través brilla un sol blanco, a través un astro negro.
Toca mi mano, esta mano que ayer sostuvo un acero:
puedes pasar en el aire, a través de ella, tus dedos!
He aquí la ausencia del hombre, la ausencia de carne, miedo,
días, cosas, almas, fuego.
Todo se quedó en el tiempo. Todo se quemó allá lejos.

Nature's husband is not with her.
The seeds of the crop haven't the strength to die,
and one hears their death like the little thread of blood that comes from the
     wounded man's mouth.
Single roses, flowers like those used in the festival of forgetfulness,
feeble odor of tombs, of grass that dies on inscribed marble.
Not a single cry. Not even the voice of a bird or a child
or the sound of a fierce assassin with his knife.
What you would give today to have your dress stained with blood!
What you would give to find some inhabited nest!
What you would give to have them plant a child in your flesh!

Finally, Lord of the Armies, here is the supreme pain.
Here, without pity, without subterfuges, without verses,
is the true pain.
At last, Lord, before us all is the pain stopped cold.
It is not a pain for the wounded, nor for the dead,
nor for the blood that was shed, nor for the earth filled with laments,
nor for the cities empty of houses, nor for the fields filled with orphans.
It is the whole pain.
There can be no tears, no sorrow,
no words, no memories.
Nothing fits now inside the chest.
All the noises of the world form one great silence.
All the men of the world form a single specter.
In the middle of this pain, soldier!, your post remains,
empty or filled.
The lives of those who are left have hollows —
complete voids —
as if they had taken mouthfuls of flesh from their bodies.
Look into this gap, the one I have here in my chest,
so you can see heavens and hells.
Look at my head. It has thousands of holes:
through it shines a white sun, through it a black star.
Touch my hand, this hand that yesterday bore steel:
you can pass your fingers through it in the air!
Here is the absence of man, the absence of flesh, fear,
days, things, souls, fire.
Everything remained in time. Everything burned over there, far away.

Juan Francisco Gutiérrez
(1920-   )

Juan Francisco Gutiérrez has suffered imprisonment and exile due to his active involvement with political groups opposed to the Somoza dictatorship. Because he has published so little of his work and lives with his family in San José, Costa Rica, Gutiérrez's poetry has, for the most part, been overlooked by his compatriots.

EL AMOR CONOCE LAS SEÑALES

Oscuros dioses inmolan detrás de cada hora,
lo que la tierra otorga. Cae, ignorado, el hombre.
Su resistencia breve relatan los suburbios,
en tono grave y sordo. Amoratados ojos
han mirado su filo doblarse como el filo de la hoja
en lívidos otoños. Y todavía esperan que liberado surja,
e ingrese en la historia. ¡La historia está ocupada
por ídolos deformes! Y arriba la muerte
arrastra las gavillas. Y las estrellas lloran.
Cuando el amor se abstuvo, estériles nubarrones
cruzaron la memoria. Sólo, el puro amor no pudo
parar bajo los pórticos los innobles propósitos.
Pero las señales conoce del elegido en ciernes.
Su imagen es distinta. ¡Buscadle en otros lechos!

LOVE KNOWS THE SIGNS

Obscure gods immolate, behind each hour,
all that the earth has granted. Man falls, ignored.
His brief resistance is told by the suburbs
in a grave, mute voice. Bruised eyes
have watched him bend like the edge of a leaf
in livid autumns. And still they hope that man
will free himself and enter history. History
is occupied by deformed idols! And above,
death drags its sheaves. And the stars cry.
When love abstained, sterile stormclouds
crossed the memory. Alone, pure love could not
stop the ignoble intentions beneath the porticos.
But it knows the signs of the chosen one in bloom.
His image is distinct. Look for him in other beds!

LA MUERTE DEL GUERRILLERO

Por conquistar la Libertad, murió el guerrero.
¡Hoy se llama nostalgia en la memoria de su pueblo!
Nosotros elegimos palabras para luchar por ella.
En su nombre nos dan hasta debajo de la lengua.
Mostrenca tierra él amaba, ahora morena le sobra.
Disueltos huesos los suyos que pisan las amapolas.
En el hostil territorio que el corazón le quemaba,
adelantársenos pudo. Reo de muerte, dejado
como un golpe eterno en la puerta de nuestra demora.
Su nombre es un nuevo canto que de noche se oye.

DEATH OF THE GUERRILLA

For conquering Liberty, the warrior died.
Today his name echoes in the memory of his people!
We choose words to fight for our freedom.
In his name they beat us even beneath our tongues.
He loved unclaimed land, now he has plenty of dark earth.
The poppies tread on his scattered bones.
In the hostile territory burned by the heart,
he helped us advance. Prisoner of death, left
like an eternal blow against the door of our delay,
his name is a new song we hear at night.

RÉQUIEM A LOS POETAS MUERTOS DE MI PATRIA

Escribieron poemas en la noche, y amaron.
No trataban de sustituir a dios alguno,
ni de imponer belleza y señorío. Tuvieron
en el corazón la cifra ardiente: Nicaragua.
La situaron exactamente, oh novia, oh incesante;
rodeándola de amor bajo la luna. Y eso basta.
Salomón, Joaquín: contra el poniente, su rostro
permanece. Rubén dijo un día que cantaban
mágicos ruiseñores dentro de sus ojos de agua.
Azaharías vió caminos sin respuestas
y Manolo los anduvo tres veces, desterrado.
La muerte ha cortado sus tendones azules, pero
la sal de la tierra brota de esos ojos cerrados.

REQUIEM FOR THE DEAD POETS OF MY COUNTRY

They wrote poems in the night, and they loved.
They didn't try to replace any god
or to impose beauty and lordliness. In their hearts
they carried the burning cipher: Nicaragua.
That's exactly where they kept her, always
surrounding her with love beneath the moon.
And that's enough. Salomón, Joaquin: against
the sunset your faces remain. Rubén said once
that magic nightingales sang in his eyes of water.
Azaharías saw roads without answers
and Manolo walked down them three times, in exile.
Death has cut their blue tendons, but
the salt of the earth sprouts from those closed eyes.

Ernesto Mejía Sánchez

(1923-   )

Ernesto Mejía Sánchez, Carlos Martínez Rivas and Ernesto Car-
denal are the principal poets of the so-called "Generation of 1940".
The preoccupation with magic and revelation in Mejía's first book,
Ensalmos y conjuros (1947) manifested itself in a rigorous, precise
poetic language. Solitude, purification, angels and fiends are some
of the themes that haunt his poetry. There is also a moralistic tone
in Mejía's work that is often the vehicle for expressing the poet's
political convictions. Mejía resurrected the prose poem in
Nicaragua, a literary form last used by Rubén Darío. Before
Ernesto Mejía Sánchez was appointed Ambassador to Spain by
Nicaragua's Government of National Reconstruction, he lived in
Mexico City and taught there at the University.

de *ENSALMOS Y CONJUROS*

*Para apaciguar la soledad, escoge
un día, virgen, Guarda todos tus libros
bajo siete llaves. Lleva una manzana
bajo el árbol más puro. No temas, no
llegará el Maligno. Dí
estas palabras, como si fuesen
verdaderas: Soledad,
te amo, creo en ti, no me traiciones.*

from INCANTATIONS AND CONJURATIONS

To pacify solitude, choose
a virgin day. Keep all your books
under seven keys. Carry an apple
under the purest tree. Do not fear,
Evil will not arrive. Say
these words, as if they were
true: Solitude,
I love you, I believe in you, do not betray me.

LA CRUZ

Infame cruz me están labrando
sin saber mi estatura.
Si grande soy la hacen pequeña
para quebrantarme los huesos;
si pequeño, altísima para
descoyuntarme. Yo mismo soy
la cruz, soy mis deseos.

THE CROSS

Infamous cross they build for me
without knowing my size.
If I am big, they make it small
to break my bones;
if small, enormous
to tear me limb from limb. I am
the cross, I am my desires.

LAS FIERAS

(JARDIN DES PLANTES)

Estamos echados sobre el césped
y no tienen piedad de nuestra dicha.
Nos espiaron ensañados. En sus ojos
no había curiosidad ni complacencia.
Envidia, sólo envidia con ira.

Nadie quiso cubrirnos ni con una
mirada de pudor. Pero
¿qué saben ellos de esto?

Querían, lo supongo, avergonzar mi amor,
el tuyo, el poco amor del mundo.
Y no pudieron con nosotros.

Jadeantes, al fin de nuestra lucha,
ahí estaban, representando el odio
que con tanto trabajo habíamos
logrado arrancar de nuestro pecho.

(Estamos solos contra ellos
pero ellos están más solos
que nosotros. A ellos no los
une ni el odio, a nosotros
hasta su odio nos reune.)

Quizá llegaron cuando yo era tu yo
y yo era tuyo. Nunca lo sabremos.
Jadeantes, saboreando, lamiendo
nuestra dicha nos encontraron. Echados
sobre el césped nos acorralaron
como fieras. Y, ahí, a sus ojos furiosos,
aterrorizados, hicimos de nuevo
nuestro fuego ya sin recato
pero imperturbable — y ellos viéndonos,
viéndonos, ignorantes y viéndonos.

THE FIENDS
(Jardin des Plantes)

We are stretched out on the grass
and they have no pity on our happiness.
They spy on us cruelly. In their eyes
there was neither curiosity nor complacency.
Envy, only envy with rage.

No one wanted to cover us with even a
modest look. But
what do they know about this?

I suppose they wanted to shame my love,
yours, the world's scarce love.
And they could not do it to us.

Panting, at the end of our fight,
there they were, representing the hatred
that with so much work we had
succeeded in ripping from our chests.

(We are alone against them
but they are more alone
than we are. Not even hatred
unites them, whereas their very
hatred keeps us together.)

Perhaps they arrived when I was your I
and I was yours. We will never know,
Panting, tasting, licking
our happiness, they found us. Stretched out
on the grass, they cornered us
like fiends. And there, before their furious,
terrified eyes, we made our fire
once again, reckless abandon
but imperturbable—and they were watching us,
watching us, unknowing and watching us.

BOLERO

Tu rostro se borra como el de la moneda en las yemas del avaro,
date prisa, y no finjas. No te conozco, pero sé lo que seas.
Sin pudor, que no hay tiempo. Que no hay tiempo fuera del
   Tiempo.
Lo que más me jode es el bien pasajero desaprovechado.

La mirada azul y oro inofensiva como de puta.
La patita blanca sin mácula, sin salud, pero blanca…
Sube, perrilla fina, hasta el lecho del moribundo…

BOLERO

Your face wears away like coins in the miser's fingers.
Hurry up, and don't fake it. I don't know you, but I know what you are.
Without modesty, because there's no time. There's no time outside
   of Time.
It really pisses me off when such good stuff is wasted.

The blue and gold look, inoffensive like a whore's.
The little white foot, unblemished, unhealthy, but white...
Come on up, you elegant bitch, to the dying man's bed...

LAS MANCHAS DEL TIGRE

¿Qué orden prescribe nuestra
congregación? Sin contorno y
sedosa la escurridiza piel
de nuestro monarca, tensa al menor
movimiento, desde adentro esculpida,
existe por nosotras. Y todo es
lanzado a la rápida ferocidad
del tirano que entigrecemos.
No se puede evitar la presencia
de nuestra escritura que dibuja
el rencor para hacerlo visible.
Decoramos lo inútil destructor,
el descenso de la bondad sin motivo.
Vamos a cuestas del resentimiento
delirante. Somos llevadas sin consulta.
No somos más que manchas. Manchas
puras llevadas y traídas por
el sin gobierno de lo sanguinario.
La belleza cargando con la culpa
de su criatura en rebeldía.

THE TIGER'S SPOTS

What order prescribes our
congregation? Without contour,
the slippery silken skin
of our monarch, tense to the slightest
movement and sculpted from within,
exists for us. And everything
is thrown at the fast and fierce
tyrant we enrage.
No one can ignore
the message we form
that makes our anger visible.
We decorate the useless destroyer,
the descent of kindness with no motive.
We burden the delirious
resentment. We are carried without being consulted.
We are nothing more than spots. Pure
spots carried and brought by
the non-government of the bloodthirsty.
Beauty bearing the blame
of its creature in rebellion.

Carlos Martínez Rivas

(1924-   )

Carlos Martínez Rivas is recognized as "the poet's poet". Due mostly to his reluctance to publish, Martínez remains unknown outside of a small, international group of writers that includes Octavio Paz. The two editions of his only book, *La insurrección solitaria* (published in Mexico in 1953 and again in Costa Rica in 1973), are both out of print. Ernesto Cardenal once said that "the best poet of our group of three is Carlos Martínez Rivas. America will know him someday." Carlos Martínez's work is marked by a verbal precision and a density or layering of meaning that is unique in Latin American poetry. José Coronel compares Martínez to César Vallejo, saying that they, in their distinct ways "are perhaps the only two modern poets in the Spanish language who have realized....important modifications in the structure of language itself." Coronel says "modern poets" because much of the "novelty" of Martínez' work is derived from the linguistic brilliance of Spanish poetry of the *Siglo de Oro*. The result is a strange convergence of Quevedo and Mallarmé, Góngora and Dylan Thomas, Calderón and T.S. Eliot. Above all, the poetry of Carlos Martínez is humanistic and compassionate. It is rooted in the everyday experiences of people from all walks of life. In many poems, the protagonists are the same kinds of social outcasts that populate the poetry of Charles Baudelaire and James Wright. Martínez is currently working in Nicaragua's agrarian reform program.

FANTASMA

Cuando, sobre los árboles, vi la trémula mano
agitarse; de la antigua bravura
de amor póstumo asilo: me volví de algun vano
inquirir arrancado, hacia la alta figura.

El apremiante "adios" las hojas repetían
para nadie; y desde siempre ininteligibles;
la luz y el lento paso de la estación, huían
ante mí por añosos cauces inaccesibles.

Cuando sobre los árboles vi el trémolo de la mano.

PHANTOM

When I saw the tremulous hand above the trees
wave; from the ancient bravura of love
posthumous haven: from some vain inquiries
I turned, diverted, toward the high shadow above.

The leaves repeated the pressing "goodbye"
for no one, from the beginning unintelligible;
I saw the season's slow step and light fly
through aged riverbeds before me, inaccessible.

When I saw the tremolo of the hand above the trees.

LAS VIRGENES PRUDENTES

... vendrá en la noche, como ladrón

¿Quién es esa mujer que canta
en la noche? ¿Quién llama a su hermana?
De país en país, esa rapsoda que vuela en el viento
por encima del mar tenebroso donde culebrea el cielo?

¡Salidle al encuentro!
Ella, la enamorada.
Ella nada más, y su hermana.
¿Ese viento que canta?

Es la voz del amor. La voz del deseo del amor que se alza
en la noche alta.
Sobre la potencia de la ciudad, esa voz que gira.
Esa aria exquisita!

Sólo esa nota vibra en la noche helada.
Esa arpa sola en la noche vasta.
Ese único silbo penetrante de la pureza.
Sólo esa serenata encantada.

Y el amor de las hermanas!
De las estrellas protegiendo sus llamas
para el Deseado que tarda.
Nada sino eso: el cañaveral de las desposadas
y la sombra alargada del Ladrón que escala.

Canta la noche y las llanuras solitarias
sometidas al hechizo de la luna. Claras,
vacías súbitamente al paso de las hermanas.
Al paso de la bandada blanca de las vírgenes hermanas.

Las que se entregaron al amor.
A quienes no se les concedió sino el amor.

Las Vírgenes Prudentes cuchicheando en la alcoba estrellada.
Bajando la voz y subiendo la llama.
Cerrándose en medio de su sombra. Desapareciendo detrás de su
    lámpara.

Aquí sólo tienes abismo. Aquí sólo hay un punto fijo:
el pábilo quieto ardiendo y el halo frío.

THE WISE VIRGINS

...he will come like a thief in the night

Who is that woman who sings
in the night? Who is calling her sister?
From country to country, that rhapsodist flying on the wind
over the murky sea where the sky slithers?

Go out to meet him!
She, the woman in love,
only she, and her sister.
That wind singing?

It is the voice of love. The voice of love's desire rising
in the high night.
Over the potency of the city, that voice spinning.
That exquisite aria!

Only that note vibrates in the frozen night.
That lonely harp in the vast night.
That single penetrating whistle of purity.
Only that bewitched serenade.

And the sisters' love!
The stars' love protecting their flames
for the Desired who is late in coming.
Nothing but that: the betrothed sisters' fields of cane
and the lengthening shadow of the climbing Thief.

The night sings and the lonely plains
beneath the spell of the moon. Suddenly
clear, empty, as the sisters pass.
As the white flock of virgin sisters passes.

Those who surrendered themselves to love.
To whom nothing was granted but love.

The Wise Virgins whispering in the starry bedroom.
Lowering their voices and raising the flame.
Closing themselves in the middle of their shadow. Disappearing
    behind their lamp.

Here you have only abyss. Here there is only one fixed point:
the quiet wick burning and the cold halo.

Aquí vas a rasgar el velo.
Aquí vas a inventar el centro.
Aquí vas a tocar el cuerpo
como toca un ciego el sueño.

Aquí podrás soplar y apagar tu secreto.

Aquí ya podrás quedarte muerto.

Here you will rip the veil.
Here you will invent the center.
Here you will touch the body
as a blind man touches the dream.

Here you may blow and put out your secret.

Here you may stay and die.

SAN CRISTÓBAL

—¿Hay paso? —gritó el niño
mirando hacia lo oscuro
en los últimos límites
de lo bruto.

Y no oyó nada, sino
la lluvia
cayendo en el abismo.

Sólo la pesantez eterna
ha respondido
honda y negra,
al niño.

—Tal vez es que no viene
nadie aquí—*cuando vió unos*
tizones apagándose,
mojados bajo el humo.

Y llamó otra vez
hacia el gran hoyo mudo.
Retó al caos palurdo.
Golpeó en su oído duro.

Y apareció un farol.
Se le acercó la noche,
cabeceando.
El pie descalzo, enorme,
removió el agua fría
y dormida.

El niño vio el reflejo del farol cruzando el río.
Sacudido
y soñoliento sobre
el alto hombro macizo.

SAINT CHRISTOPHER

"Is there some way across?" shouted the child
looking toward the dark
in the ultimate limits
of brutishness.

And he heard nothing but
the rain
falling in the abyss.

Only the eternal heaviness
has responded,
deep and black,
to the child.

*"Maybe no one
comes here"*—then he saw
some embers die down,
wet beneath the smoke.

And he called again
toward the great mute hole.
He challenged the rustic chaos.
He struck its hard ear.

And a lantern appeared.
Night drew closer to him,
nodding.
The bare foot, enormous,
stirred the cold and sleeping
water.

And the child saw the lantern's reflection
crossing the river.
Shaken
and drowsy on
the high massive shoulder.

BESO PARA LA MUJER DE LOT

"Y su mujer, habiendo vuelto la vista atrás,
trocóse en columna de sal."

Génesis. XIX:26

Dime tú algo más.

¿Quién fue ese amante que burló al bueno de Lot
y quedó sepultado bajo el arco
caído y la ceniza? ¿Qué
dardo te traspasó certero, cuando oiste
a los dos ángeles
recitando la preciosa nueva del perdón
para Lot y los suyos?

¿Enmudeciste pálida, suprimida; o fuiste
de aposento en aposento, fingiéndole
un rostro al regocijo de los justos y la prisa
de las sirvientas, sudorosas y limitadas?

Fue después que se hizo más difícil fingir.

Cuando marchabas detrás de todos,
remolona, tardía. Escuchando
a lo lejos el silbido y el trueno, mientras
el aire del castigo
ya rozaba tu suelta cabellera entrecana.

Y te volviste.

Extraño era, en la noche, esa parte
abierta del cielo chisporroteando.
Casi alegre el espanto. Cohetes sobre Sodoma.
Oro y carmesí cayendo
sobre la quilla de la ciudad a pique.

Hacia allá partían como flechas tus miradas,
buscando… Y tal vez lo viste. Porque el ojo
de la mujer reconoce a su rey
aun cuando las naciones tiemblen y los cielos lluevan fuego.

KISS FOR LOT'S WIFE

"But his wife looked back from behind him,
and she became a pillar of salt."

Genesis. XIX: 26

Tell me something else.

Who was that lover who tricked good Lot
and lies buried beneath the
fallen arch and ash? What
well-aimed dart pierced you, when you heard
the two angels
reciting the precious news of the pardon
for Lot and his people?

Were you speechless, pale, supressed; or did you go
from chamber to chamber, feigning
a face for the rejoicing of the just and the haste
of the handmaidens, sweaty and limited?

It was afterwards that it became more difficult to pretend.

When you lagged behind them all,
unwilling and slow. Listening
to the whistle and the thunder in the distance, while
the air of the punishment
grazed your loose graying hair.

And you turned.

It was strange, in the night, that open
part of the sky sparking.
Almost joyous the fright. Fireworks over Sodom.
Gold and crimson falling
over the keel of the sinking city.

Over there, where your glances sped like arrows,
searching... And perhaps you saw him. Because
a woman recognizes her king
even when nations tremble and the skies rain fire.

Toda la noche, ante tu cabeza cerrada
de estatua, llovió azufre y fuego sobre Sodoma
y Gomorra. Al alba, con el sol, la humareda
subía de la tierra como el vaho de un horno.

Así colmaste la copa de la iniquidad.
Sobrepasando el castigo.
Usurpándolo a fuerza de desborde.

Era preciso hundirse, con el ídolo
estúpido y dorado, con los dátiles,
el decacordio
y el ramito con hojas del cilantro.

¡Para no renacer!
Para que todo duerma, reducido a perpetuo
montón de ceniza. Sin que surja
de allí ningún Fénix aventajado.

Si todo pasó así, Señora, y yo
he acertado contigo, eso no lo sabremos.

Pero una estatua de sal no es una Musa inoportuna.

Una esbelta reunión de minúsculas
entidades de sal corrosiva,
es cristaloides. Acetato. Aristas
de expresión genuina. Y no la riente
colina aderezada por los ángeles.

La sospechosamente siempreverdeante Söar
con el blanco y senil Lot, y las dos chicas
núbiles, delicadas y puercas.

All night long, before your head
sealed like a statue's, it rained fire and brimstone over Sodom
and Gomorrah. At dawn, with the sun, the cloud of smoke
rose from the earth like vapor from an oven.

That is how you filled the cup of iniquity.
By exceeding the punishment,
usurping it, overflowing with it yourself.

You had to sink with the stupid, golden
idol, with the date-fruit,
the decachord,
and the twigs of coriander.

So as not to be reborn!
So that everything sleeps, reduced to a perpetual
pile of ash from which
no beneficial Phoenix will arise.

If it all happened like this, Milady, and I
have stumbled upon you, that we will never know.

But a statue of salt is not an inopportune Muse.

A slender assemblage of minuscule
entities of corrosive salt,
in crystalloids. Acetate. Edges
of genuine expression. And not the cheerful
hill prepared by angels.

The suspiciously evergreening Zoar
with the white and senile Lot, and the two girls,
nubile, delicate, and piggish.

DOS MURALES U.S.A.

A Ángel Martínez Baigoirri, S. J.
Tributo al maestro

I

LA MUERTE ENTRANTE

(MURAL DIURNO)

> Un espíritu me pasó por delante,
> los pelos de mi carne se erizaron;
>   plantóse un espectro ante mis ojos,
> y no reconocí su rostro.
>
> *ELIFAZ EL TEMANITA.*

1

Mientras que prisionero de las escalerillas
de escape,
                los patios pozos
                                y las asquerosas
cremas en pie de querubín;
bajo la alta pública mecida cuna de luz
                en va y ven;
por la batiente lámina de reflejo y ráfaga

                entras:
en sandalia la planta pie celeste.
A mano grande como pie abierto como risa.
                Suelta
la crin de púrpura y herrumbre,
                greñas
amparando la negligencia del siglo.
                Tintorera
te sientas cruzada a tranca y signo:
X Sables Cerrojo agujas de tejer en ovillo.

                Te pliegas
a azotar el suelo con la suela
de palo a añudar la hedionda correa
que estranguló el pulgar uñavioleta.

TWO MURALS: U.S.A.

to Ángel Martínez Baigoirri, S.J.
Tribute to the master.

I

THE UPCOMING DEATH

(DIURNAL MURAL)

> Then a spirit passed before my face;
> the hair of my flesh stood up:
> it stood still, but I could not
> discern the form thereof:
> an image was before mine eyes.
>
> ELIPHAZ THE TEMANITE

1

While prisoner of fire-
escapes,
                    courtyards like wells
                              and nauseating
ice cream cones reached for by cherubs on tiptoe;
under the high   public   swinging cradle of light
                              endlessly rocking;
through the flapping lamina of reflection and wind

                    you step in:
on sandaled sole of celestial foot.
Big-handed as foot open like laughter.
                    Loose
rust-colored purple mane,
                    mophead
concealing the century's negligence.
                    Shark-woman, user of dyes
you sit down cross-bar as omen:
X   Sabres   Bolt   knitting needles in ball of yarn.

                    You stoop
to whip the floor with wooden sole
to tie the stinking strap
that strangled the violetnail toe.

2

Si arqueado lomo asume curva
de la convexa desventura
talón legible pende
y pesa sobre el centro de la
                    Esfera.

                                    A prudente
distancia tu cautivo
incógnito espío ese
talón. El mismo
callo pulido criso
elefantino
machacasesos
que ya supimos.

Tampoco me son extraños estos
                    peñascos.
Tales acantilados.
Reconozco esos escollos
llameando apagándose extraviándome
llamándome uno desde el otro
            —Caribdis desde Escila—
                con laringilla
de luciérnaga y soplo.

El sarro el motëado el itinerario
de orugas en fila india bajo
la hojosa humedad

                                    (Taumato
poea processionea)

                            No me son ajenas

aquestas pecas

la tórrida desolación la arena
del mediodía el sol mosqueado
de pepescas muertas en la cesta
y el sedal y la red y la ristra
de huevecillos y la lona nacida

2

If arched back assumes curve
of the convex misfortune
legible heel hangs
and weighs over the center of the
                                    Sphere.

                                    At a prudent
distance your unknown captive
spies that
heel. The same
callus polished bolden
elephant-ivory
brainmasher
that we already knew.

Nor do these chunks of rock
                    seem strange to me.
Such cliffs.
I recognize those reefs
flaming stifling leading me astray
calling me one from the other
                —Charybdis from Scylla—
                    with tiny larynx
of firefly and puff of wind.

The rust the pied the itinerary
of silkworms in Indian file beneath
the leafy dampness
                        (Taumato
poea processionea)
                    To mine eyes
these freckles are not another's

the torrid desolation   the sand
at noon   the fly-befouled sun
of dead minnows in the basket
and the fishing line and net and string
of tiny eggs and the moldy canvas

y el chiqüije
            (¡de memoria esos arrecifes!)

resumo: he visto esas escarpadas espaldas de mujer
a merced
mía soltándose las medias a la entrada de un lecho
donde ya espero.

                        3

                                            Pero
no te conozco Máscara désta Muerte CARATULA
                    ESMERALDA
                    TOPACIO
¡huy, ROJA! ¿quién es eso? espectro para
la fertilización del pánico.

                                (No el viejo
miedo sino verde césped. Césped
más nuevo que el cielo, más fresco
que el cielo como césped verde.
El chorro jardinero tableteando girando niñas
con regaderas regando el pánico y la
cortadora de césped haciendo césped más tierno
que el verde cielo del césped del cielo
verde verdeando los lozanos vastos
altos pastos del pánico

el que viene el entrante el consentido el mimado
de la alborada. No anunciado
aún en el Cartel que un metro más pequeño
que el Cielo amanece. Pero más nuevo ¡ah, eso
sí! húmedo sin pájaros en blanco.

Sólo el vacante anuncio sin anuncio.
El pálido empapelado rectángulo.
La escoba de estopa el cubo del engrudo
el largo andamio solitario.)

and the fishy smell
                    (those reefs by heart!)

to summarize: I have seen the crags of backs of women
at my mercy
rolling down their stockings on the edge of a bed
where already I am waiting.

                            3

                                                But
I do not know you Mask of this Death   FALSE-FACE
                            EMERALD
                            TOPAZ
huy, RED! Who is that? Specter for
the fertilization of panic.

                            (Not the good old
fear but the green lawn. Lawn
newer than the sky, fresher
than the sky as green lawn.
The garden sprinkler ticking spinning   little girls
with watering cans watering the panic and the
lawnmower making the lawn younger
than the green sky of the lawn of the green sky
greening the vast burgeoning
lofty pastures of panic

the next the upcoming the favorite the minion
of daybreak. Unannounced
yet on the Billboard that dawns
one meter smaller than the Sky. But newer ah, that
yes! damp   without birds   blank.

Only the vacant advertisement with no message.
The pale papered rectangle.
The brush of tow   the bucket of paste
the large lonely platform.)

4

Te desconozco.

Rezongas y te revuelves a lo durmiente
de tres perfiles y cinco codos.
Farfulla amordazada con alfileres
tu modista maldita
midiéndote con la sierpe amarilla
mordiendo el agraz del pecho la espina
del flanco
bermeja hermana de Lilith árbol
de la muerte higuera seca calcinado
agavanzo.

5

Pero injértame
en la esquina
viva.
Aprieta
las rodillas
de cráneos de mellizas.
Cierra las piernas
cierra las tijeras
de la Parca.

Prénseme la trampa
de tu hueso. Sienta
la presión de tu muerte. Sepa
el grado exacto de prensilidad de la
muerte encarnada
de la carne descarnada
de tu esqueleto escarlata.

4

I do not recognize you.

You grumble and return to the sleeping
of three profiles and five elbows.
Your damn dressmaker
sputters gagged with pins
measuring you with the yellow serpent
biting the bitter grapes of the chest   the thorn
of the flank
vermilion sister of Lilith   tree
of death   dry fig-tree   calcinated
rosebush.

5

But graft me
onto the living
corner.
Press together
the knees
of twin girls' skulls.
Close the legs
close the scissors
of Fate.

Let the trap of your bone
squeeze me. So I feel
the pressure of your death. So I know
the exact degree of prehensility of
death made flesh
of death unfleshed
of your scarlet skeleton.

6

—¿Y viste, así que se fué, el si-
tio sucio de sangre y polvo?

                                        Sí.

Y pensé: de temer es
pueblo de tales mujeres.
Y pensé en la hija de Merarí, Judit,
                        en el Dios
que herirá por mano de mujer, en que
visiones así confirman
                        nos
que lo Peor está y aún no acaece.

II

AQUÍ FALTA LA PIEDRA

(MURAL NOCTURNO)

1

        Ajeno en la respiración ajena atravieso
noche sin piedra
                                lejos
un ángulo de cielo relampaguea
                                una
                        estrella se cruza
                                de un agujero
a otro
                                fragmento
de astro trozo
de tiza en lo pizarroso

2

                                                STOP

ROAD
CLOSED

6

— And did you see, since she has gone,
the dirty place of blood and dust?
                              Yes.
And I thought: it is worth fearing
a town of such women.
And I thought of Merari's daughter, Judith,
                              of the God
that wounds by woman's hand, of
the visions confirming
                    to us
that the Worst is here and yet to come.

II

HERE STONE IS LACKING

(NOCTURNAL MURAL)

1

Alienated in the alienated breathing I cross
night without stone
                              far away
an angle of sky flashes
                    one
                    star crosses
                    from one hole
to another
                    astral
fragment   piece
of chalk in the slatish

2

                              STOP

ROAD
CLOSED

(cerco de estrictos parpadeantes
fuegos fatuos

                maderamen
                  escombros
                     fosos

falsas tumbas que abriera
simulacro
de piedrasobrepiedra)

3

Aquí, en cada esquina
día a día
todo el año

al sol
ensordecedor

el taladro
horada
la cáscara
de asfalto

perfora
buscando
roca

halla sólo
turrón poroso

alza polvo
semanal

4

¡Ay,
en verdad, más te valiera Padre dar
al hijo que te pidiere aquí
                pan,
una piedra! Un adoquín

(roadblock of strict blinking
will o'the wisps

                              lumber
                              rubbish
                              holes

       false tombs that would be opened
       semblance
of stoneonstone)

3

Here, on every corner
day after day
all year long

in the sun
deafening

the jackhammer
drills
the shell
of asphalt

perforates
searching for
rock

finds only
porous nougat

raises weekly
dust

4

Ay,
in truth, it would be worth more Father to give
your son who begged you here for
                        bread,
a stone! A flagstone

que roer en vez
de miga de papel
                    PADRE
nuestro que estás, que eres, dale
                    a tu hijo
un raigón angular, fresca

        cantera.
Una baldosa de atrio
para el tacón, su retiñido
para el tímpano ¡tanto
pedir! Una astilla de granito
        para Sísifo,
un guijarro adecuado a sus hábitos.

                    5

¡Y dormir! laja sobre bloque, dolmen
donde para morir ese segundo
hondo de nada y sueño de la vida.

En alianza con las secretas inextricables
apresuradas vertientes (aunque
espera: más bien lentas...¡Sí! veneros
fluyendo apenas un poco más lentos que el tiempo),

piedra contra la piedra.
Puesto el oído en el profundo
callar de su corazón acueducto,
mientras los últimos jirones
de temor se demoran en nuestra carne.

Que de noche
tenemos miedo porque falta
la piedra. Y da pavor el cartón.
La ciudad de cajas
vacías. Su rumor
solitario
de papel carcomido por cucarachas.

to gnaw on instead
of crumbs of paper
             our FATHER
who art, you who are, give
                   your son
an angular molar root, fresh

      quarry.
Atrium flagstone
for the heel, its ringing echo
for the eardrum, so much
to demand! A splinter of granite
             for Sisyphus,
a cobblestone appropriate for his habits.

5

And to sleep! slab on block, dolmen,
a place to die that deep second
of life's nothing and dream.

Allied with secrets, inextricable
hurried secrets, cascading (but
wait, rather slowly ... Yes! fountains
flowing just a little slower than time),

stone against the stone.
The ear placed on the profound
silence of its aqueduct heart,
with the last shreds of fear
lingering within our flesh.

Thence by night
we are afraid because stone
is lacking. And cardboard causes dread.
The city of empty boxes. Its lonely
murmur
of paper gnawed by cockroaches.

6

            ¿Acaso
aquí, el grito
del vendedor; el silbido
de la ramera; el toc
        toc
            del cojo;
                los arrastriscos
contrahechos en sus muñones, como
candelabros arrumbados;

                        ¿acaso
el pobrecito hablador;
la miseria y su tonadilla — *digo,*
su desdentado hueco músico — *halló*
pérdida
pozo
eco en la colmenar oreja vacía de la piedra?

            — *No.*
Entonces ¿quién entonces, quiso
cantar LA PIEDRA aquí?
Piedra qué? cuál? ¿Piedra la arcilla, piedra
la cal la arena la alta rueda
                    don-
de el hormigón
            golpea?

            ¡*Yo*
                dije
PIEDRA
        PIERRE
            STONE
            SASSO
STEINNNNN!

                    Quise
querría creo querer decir la roca Cristo
la piedra Pedro el empedrado patio el pretorio

6

Perhaps
here, the cry
of the vendor; the whistle
of the harlot; the *toc*
        toc
            of the lame;
                        the dragging
deformed on their stumps, like
candelabra cast aside;
                        perhaps
the little babbler about town;
misery and its strain—I say,
its toothless musician hollow—found
loss
pit
echo in the empty beehive-ear of stone?

                                —No.

Then, who then, attempted
to sing THE STONE here?
What stone? Which one? Is it stone the clay, stone
the ash the sand the high wheel
                        where
the gravel
        rumbles?

                I
                    said
STONE
        PIERRE
                PIEDRA
                SASSO
STEINNNNN!

                        I tried
I would want I think I want to say the rock Christ
the stone Peter the paved courtyard the praetorian

el canto

                    del peldaño
el canto

                    rodado
el canto

                    del gallo
y los sollozos

Los amargos largos sollozos

the edge
                    of the step
the rolling
                    cobblestone
the cock's
                    cry
and the sobs

The bitter long sobs

Ernesto Cardenal

(1925-   )

Ernesto Cardenal's poetry, which has been translated into more than fifteen languages, embraces all of the Americas. Cardenal freely acknowledges his debt to certain North American poets, especially Whitman, Pound and Merton. Cardenal's language can be visionary, beautiful in its clarity, and readily accessible to people of diverse educational backgrounds. One finds in the immediacy of recent poetry by Cardenal a real social and political value that enables the poet to take part in the collective process of a people realizing their dream of self-determination. Cardenal is the main proponent of *la poesía exteriorista* which is, in his words, "the only poetry that can express Latin American reality, reach the people, and be revolutionary." After Somoza's National Guard destroyed his legendary community on the island of Solentiname, Cardenal devoted all his efforts to the Nicaraguan revolution as poet, radical priest, spokesman for the *Frente Sandinista,* and Minister of Culture.

TAHIRASSAWICHI EN WASHINGTON

En 1898 Tahirassawichi fue a Washington
"solamente para hablar de religión"
                    (como dijo al gobierno americano)
            solamente para preservar las oraciones.
Y no le impresionó el Capitolio.
La Biblioteca del Congreso estaba bien
pero no servía para guardar los objetos sagrados
que sólo podían guardarse en su choza de barro
            (que se estaba cayendo).
Cuando en el monumento a Washington le preguntaron
si quería subir por el ascensor o las escaleras
contestó: "No subiré. Los blancos amontonan piedras
para subir a ellas. Yo no subiré.
        Yo he subido a las montañas hechas por Tirawa".
Y Tahirassawichi dijo al Departamento de Estado:
"La Choza de Tirawa es el redondo cielo azul
            (no nos gusta que haya nubes entre Tirawa y nosotros)
Lo primero que hay que hacer
es escoger un lugar sagrado para habitar
un lugar consagrado a Tirawa, donde el hombre
pueda estar en silencio y meditación.
Nuestra choza redonda representa el nido
            (el nido donde estar juntos y guardar los hijitos)
En el centro está el fuego que nos une en una sola familia.
La puerta es para que cualquiera pueda entrar
y es por donde entran las visiones.
El azul es el color de la Choza de Tirawa
y mezclamos tierra azul con agua de río
porque el río representa la vida que corre
sin parar, a través de las generaciones.
La olla de la pintura azul es la comba del cielo
y pintamos una mazorca, que es el poder de la tierra.
Pero ese poder le viene de arriba, de Tirawa
por eso pintamos la mazorca con el color de Tirawa.
Después ofrecemos a Tirawa humo de tabaco.
            Antes no se fumaba por placer sino sólo por oración
            los blancos enseñaron a la gente a profanar el tabaco.
En el camino saludamos a todas las cosas con cantos
porque Tirawa está en todas las cosas. Saludamos los ríos:
desde lejos los ríos son una línea de árboles

TAHIRASSAWICHI IN WASHINGTON

In 1898 Tahirassawichi went to Washington
"only to speak about religion"
           (as he said to the American government)
        only to preserve the prayers.
And the Capitol did not impress him.
The Library of Congress was all right
but it did not serve to keep the sacred objects
that only could be kept in their mud lodge
                    (that was falling down).
When they asked him at the Washington Monument
if he wanted to take the elevator or the stairs
he replied: "I will not go up. The white man makes piles of stones
to go up them. I will not go up.
        I have gone up the mountains made by Tirawa."
And Tahirassawichi said to the Department of State:
"Tirawa's Lodge is the round blue sky
    (we do not like it when there are clouds between Tirawa and us)
The first thing that has to be done
is to choose a sacred place to live,
a place consecrated to Tirawa, where man
can live in silence and meditation.
Our round lodge represents the nest
        (the nest where we can be together and keep the small children)
In the center is the fire that joins us into a single family.
The door is for anyone to enter
and for visions to enter.
Blue is the color of Tirawa's Lodge
and we mix blue earth with riverwater
because the river represents the life that flows
without stopping, through the generations.
The pot of blue paint is the dome of the sky
and we paint an ear of corn that is the power of the earth.
But that power comes from above, from Tirawa.
That is why we paint the corn the color of Tirawa.
Then we offer tobacco smoke to Tirawa.
        Before, one did not smoke for pleasure, only in prayer.
        The white man taught the people to profane tobacco.
On the paths we greet all things with songs,
because Tirawa is in all things. We greet the rivers:
from far away the rivers are a line of trees

y cantamos a esos árboles
más cerca vemos la línea de agua, y la oímos sonar
y cantamos al agua que corre sonando.
Y cantamos a los búfalos, pero no en las praderas
el Canto de los Búfalos lo cantamos en la choza
porque ya no hay búfalos.
Y cantamos las montañas, que fueron hechas por Tirawa.
A las montañas subimos solos, cuando vamos a rezar.
Desde allí se ve si hay enemigos. También si vienen amigos.
Las montañas son buenas para el hombre por eso las cantamos.
Y cantamos las mesetas, pero las cantamos en la choza
porque nosotros no hemos visto mesetas
            esas montañas planas en la cumbre
pero nos han dicho que nuestros padres veían muchas mesetas
y recordamos lo que vieron allá lejos, en sus viajes.
Y cantamos a la aurora cuando sale del oriente
y toda la vida se renueva
(esto es muy misterioso, les estoy hablando
            de algo muy sagrado)
Cantamos al lucero de la mañana
el lucero es como un hombre y está pintado de rojo
            el color de la vida.
Cantamos cuando se despiertan los animales
y salen de sus escondites donde estaban dormidos.
La venada sale primero, seguida de su venadito.
Cantamos cuando entra el sol en la puerta de la choza
y cuando llega al borde del tragaluz en el centro de la choza
y después en la tarde cuando ya no hay sol en la choza
y está en el borde de las montañas que son como la pared
de una gran choza redonda donde viven los pueblos.
Cantamos en la noche cuando vienen los sueños.
Porque las visiones nos visitan más fácilmente de noche.
Viajan más fácilmente por la tierra dormida.
Se acercan a la choza y se paran en la puerta
y después entran en la choza, llenándola toda.
Si no fuera verdad que vinieran esos sueños
hace tiempo que habríamos abandonado los cantos.
Y cantamos en la noche cuando salen las Pléyades.
Las siete estrellas están siempre juntas
y orientan al que está perdido, lejos de su aldea

and we sing those trees
closer, we see the line of water, and we hear its sound
and we sing the water that flows with its song.
And we sing the buffaloes, but not on the prairies.
We sing the *Song of the Buffaloes* in the lodge
because there are no longer any buffaloes.
And we sing the mountains because Tirawa made them.
We go alone up the mountains when we wish to pray.
From there one sees if there are enemies. Or if friends are coming.
The mountains are good for man, that is why we sing them.
And we sing the mesas, but we sing them in the lodge
because we have not seen mesas,
      those mountains flat on top
but they have told us that our fathers saw many mesas
and we remember what they saw so far away in their journeys.
And we sing the dawn when it comes in the east
and all life renews itself
(this is very mysterious, I speak to you
      of something very sacred)
We sing the morning star
the star is like a man and is painted red,
      the color of life.
We sing when the animals wake
and come from their hiding places where they slept.
The doe come first, followed by her fawn.
We sing when the sun enters the door of the lodge
and when it reaches the edge of the skylight in the center of the lodge
and later in the afternoon when there is no sun in the lodge
and the sun is on the edge of the mountains that are like a wall
of a great round lodge where all the people live.
We sing in the night when dreams come.
Because visions visit us more easily at night.
They travel more easily over the sleeping earth.
They draw near the lodge, filling it completely.
If it were not the truth that those dreams came
we would have abandoned the songs a long time ago.
And we sing in the night when the Pleiades rise.
The seven stars are always together
and guide the one who is lost, far from his village

(y enseñan a los hombres a estar unidos como ellas).
Tirawa es el padre de todos nuestros sueños
y prolonga nuestra tribu a través de los hijos.
Con el agua azul pintamos el signo de Tirawa
(un arco y en su centro una recta que baja)
en el rostro de un niño.
       El arco en la frente y las mejillas
       y la línea recta, en la nariz.
(el archo es la comba azul donde vive Tirawa
y la línea recta su aliento que baja y nos da vida).
El rostro del niño representa la nueva generación
y el agua de río es el pasar de las generaciones
y la tierra azul que mezclamos es el cielo de Tirawa
(y el dibujo azul así trazado es el rostro de Tirawa).
Después hacemos al niño mirar agua de río
y él al mirar el agua ve también su propia imagen
como viendo en su rostro sus hijos y los hijos de sus hijos
pero está viendo también el rostro azul de Tirawa
retratado en su rostro y en las futuras generaciones.
Nuestra choza les dije tiene forma de nido
y si suben a una montaña y miran alrededor
verán que el cielo rodea toda la tierra
y la tierra es redonda y tiene forma de nido
para que todas las tribus vivan juntas y unidas.
La tormenta puede botar el nido del águila
pero el nido de la oropéndola sólo se mece en el viento
       y no le pasa nada".

Tahirassawichi, supongo, para el Departamento de Estado no ha
   dicho nada.

(and they teach man to be as united as they are).
Tirawa is the father of all our dreams
and prolongs the tribe through our children.
With blue water we paint the sign of Tirawa
(an arch and in its center a descending line)
on the face of a child.
    The arch on the forehead and the cheeks
    and the straight line on the nose.
(the arch is the blue dome where Tirawa lives
and the straight line his breath that descends and gives us life).
The face of the child represents the new generation
and the riverwater is the passing of generations
and the blue earth that we mix is Tirawa's sky
(and the blue drawing drawn like this is Tirawa's face).
Later, we make the child watch the riverwater
and he, watching the water, sees his own image as well
as seeing in his face his children and his children's children,
but he is also seeing Tirawa's blue face
portrayed in his face and in the future generations.
Our lodge, I told you, is shaped like a nest
and if you go up a mountain and look around you
you will see that the sky surrounds all the land
and the land is round and is shaped like a nest
so that all the tribes can live together in unity.
The storm can knock down the eagle's nest
but the nest of the golden oriole only rocks in the wind and nothing
    happens to it."

Tahirassawichi, I suppose, has said nothing to the Department of
    State.

LA CIUDAD DESHABITADA

(fragmento)

   Sitiada por las muertes de todas sus tardes para siempre,
en aquella tierra blanca como la sal en que fué establecida,
blanca como la sed, en la desolación del sol,
y el estertor de un lago que al medio día se siente de ceniza,
impasible, impasible, hasta su más alejado horizonte,
como una losa perfectamente ajustada al infinito,
y las olas como recorriendo un cementerio incesante,
frecuentemente solitario recuerdo todas sus calles,
frecuentemente durmiendo mi cuerpo otra vez las ha recorrido,
y así de noche enteramente blanca emerge,
en medio de la tierra en que ha sido edificada su ruina.
Sitiada por el polvo, por el tiempo que lentamente invade en la piedra
una ciudad derrotada de la que es necesario salir,
porque aquí una ceniza definitiva ha entrado al asalto,
porque aquí no queda nada y es necesario partir,
es necesario partir. Pero algo regresa
en ciertas edades inexplicables poco después de la lluvia,
o cuando dormimos bajo firmamentos ausentes hace tiempo,
o recomenzamos un diálogo hace años inconcluso,
algo regresa, algo no puede definitivamente partir
y así llamamos conmovidos a alguna puerta querida
que se abría al atardecer a un centenar de sueños de amor.

        .   .   .   .

   Recordemos a Hernández de Córdoba en la costa estridente del lago
trazando el sueño de esta ciudad con tanta pasión edificada,
al Conquistador diciendo: "Esta tierra bronceada será mi mujer para
      siempre",
construyendo en un territorio disputado palmo a palmo con los tigres,
y todo esto para qué, si el polvo voraz desata su ofensiva,
si la mujer y la planta van creciendo vertiginosamente hacia la muerte
y la columna de mármol se marchita igual que una camelia blanca;
si la ceniza levanta su tallo invasor más alto que las torres,
más alto inclusive que unos labios inconmovibles que besan,
y esta ciudad es tan sólo la osamenta reluciente de una gran ilusión,

THE UNINHABITED CITY
(fragment)

Besieged by the deaths of all its afternoons forever,
in that land white as salt in which it was founded,
white as thirst in the desolation of the sun,
and the death rattle of a lake that feels like ash at noon,
impassive, impassive to its most distant horizon,
like a slab of stone adjusted perfectly to the infinite,
and the waves passing through an incessant graveyard,
frequently lonely I remember its streets,
frequently sleeping my body once again walks them all,
and thus by night, completely white, it emerges,
in the middle of the land where its ruin has been built.
Besieged by dust, by time that slowly invades the stone:
a defeated city we must leave,
because here a definite ash has entered the assault,
because here nothing remains and we must leave,
it is necessary to leave. But something returns
in certain inexplicable ages just after the rain,
or when we sleep beneath firmaments absent a long time ago,
or once again we begin a dialogue for many years unfinished,
something returns, nothing can definitely leave
and so, deeply moved, we called to some beloved door
that opened in the late afternoon to a hundred dreams of love.

.   .   .   .

Let us remember Hernández de Córdoba on the strident coast of the lake
drawing the dream of this city with such edified passion,
saying to the Conquistador: "This bronzed land will be my woman
     forever,"
building on a territory, disputing it inch by inch with the tigers.
and all this for what, if the voracious dust lets loose its offensive,
if the woman and the plant keep growing dizzily toward death
and the marble column withers just like a camellia;
if the ashes lift their invader's stem higher than the towers,
or even higher than some unmoved lips that kiss,
and this city is only the brilliant skeleton of some grand illusion,
an assembly of the dead over which the shadow of a

una asamblea de muertos presidida por la sombra de un conquistador
    ya degollado,
donde antiguas cabelleras en forma de cocoteros o de olas gimen bajo los
    astros.
Invito a todos los que se acogen al abrigo de estos muros de muerte,
a todos los que lloran en esta margen por un país de amor y eternidades,
a todos los que agonizan sobre femeninas dunas calcinadas,
invito a hacer un viaje, más allá de donde el mar levanta su humareda,
más allá del horizonte donde el ataúd del mundo definitivamente
    se cierra
bajo el peso de un cielo insostenible hecho de lápidas azules;
invito a hacer un viaje, muy lejos de esta tierra, de esta ciudad y su
    mortaja,
antes que la última embarcación se marchite cercada por el polvo,
porque es necesario partir, porque es necesario partir.

conquistador whose throat has already been slit presides,
where ancient heads of hair in the form of coconut trees or waves
    moan beneath the stars.
I invite all those who seek shelter from these walls of death,
all those who cry on this margin for a country of love and eternities,
all those who agonize on feminine sun-bleached dunes,
I invite all of you to take a journey, beyond where the sea lifts its
    cloud of smoke,
beyond the horizon where the coffin of the world is sealed shut
beneath the weight of an unbearable sky of blue stone tablets;
I invite you to take a journey, far from this earth, from this city and
    its shroud,
before the last embarkation withers, encircled by dust,
because we must leave, because we must leave.

MANAGUA 6:30 P.M.

En las tardes son dulces los neones
y las luces de mercurio pálidas y bellas...
y la estrella roja de una torre de radio
en el cielo crepuscular de Managua
es tan bonita como Venus
y un anuncio ESSO es como la luna

Las lucecitas rojas de los automóviles son místicas
(el alma es como una muchacha besuqueada detrás de un auto)
    TACA BUNGE KLM SINGER
    MENNEN HTM GOMEZ NORGE
    RPM SAF OPTICA SELECTA
proclaman la gloria de Dios!
(Bésame bajo los anuncios luminosos oh Dios)
    KODAK TROPICAL RADIO F&C REYES
en muchos colores
deletrean tu Nombre.
                "Trasmiten
la noticia..."
Otro significado
no lo conozco
Las crueldades de esas luces no las defiendo
Y si he de dar un testimonio sobre mi época
es éste: Fue bárbara y primitiva
pero poética.

MANAGUA 6:30 P.M.

In the afternoons the neon lights are sweet
and the mercury lights, pale and beautiful...
and the radio tower's red star
in Managua's sky at dusk
is as pretty as Venus
and an ESSO advertisement is like the moon

the little red lights of the cars are mystical
(the soul is like a girl being kissed behind a car)
   TACA BUNGE KLM SINGER
   MENNEN HTM GOMEZ NORGE
   RPM SAF OPTICA SELECTA
they proclaim the glory of God!
(Kiss me beneath the luminous advertisements O God)
   KODAK TROPICAL RADIO F&C REYES
in many colors
they spell your Name.
                   "They transmit
the news..."
Another meaning
I do not know
I do not defend the cruelties of these lights
and if I were to give testimony about my epoch
it would be this: It was barbaric and primitive
but poetic.

SOMOZA DESVELIZA LA ESTATUA DE SOMOZA
EN EL ESTADIO SOMOZA

No es que yo crea que el pueblo me erigió esta estatua
porque yo sé mejor que vosotros que la ordené yo mismo.
Ni tampoco que pretenda pasar con ella a la posteridad
porque yo sé que el pueblo la derribará un dia.
Ni que haya querido erigirme a mí mismo en vida
el monumento que muerto no me erigiréis vosotros:
sino que erigí esta estatua porque sé que la odiáis.

SOMOZA UNVEILS THE STATUE OF SOMOZA
IN SOMOZA STADIUM

It's not that I think the people erected this statue
because I know better than you that I ordered it myself.
Nor do I pretend to pass into posterity with it
because I know the people will topple it over someday.
Not that I wanted to erect to myself in life
the monument you never would erect to me in death:
I erected this statue because I knew you would hate it.

Ernesto Gutiérrez

(1929-   )

Ernesto Gutiérrez is the most consistent and accomplished poet of
the Generation of 1950. In 1980, he was a member of the panel of
judges at the prestigious *Casa de las Américas* awards for litera-
ture. His poetry and essays have won prizes in Latin America and
Europe. Before his appointment as Nicaragua's ambassador to
Brazil, Gutiérrez taught at the National Autonomous University of
Nicaragua in León where he was also in charge of the most distin-
guished publishing house in the country.

LOS COLORES

Negro:
   Negra es la guerra
   y negra es la muerte
   porque negro es el cuchillo de obsidiana
   con que tienes que matar.

Amarillo:
   Amarillo es el sol
   y amarillo es el maíz
   fuentes de toda vida.

Rojo:
   es el color de la energía y del valor
   porque roja es la sangre de la madre
   y roja también la sangre del guerrero.

Azul:
   es el color del sacrificio
   porque todo sacrificio es religioso
   y azul es el color del cielo.

Verde:
   verde es el color de la realeza
   porque verde es el color del quetzal
   y sus plumas son exclusivas
   para los nobles y los jefes.

THE COLORS

Black:
>   War is black
>   and death is black
>   because black is the obsidian knife
>   you must use to kill.

Yellow:
>   The sun is yellow
>   and the corn is yellow —
>   sources of all life.

Red:
>   It is the color of energy and bravery
>   because the mother's blood is red
>   and so is the blood of the warrior.

Blue:
>   It is the color of sacrifice
>   because all sacrifice is religious
>   and blue is the color of the sky.

Green:
>   Green is the color of royalty
>   because green is the color of the quetzal
>   and its feathers are exclusively
>   for the nobles and the chiefs.

LA INSISTENCIA NO SEDUCE, RINDE

Cada día tiene su propia
significación
y el año gira
cargado de recuerdos

Dichoso aquél
que a su virtud confía
la abrumadora ejecución
de la vida diaria

Yo he tratado de
he insistido en
pero sólo con mi parte
no basta para un amor
entre los dos

Y esta creciente vaciedad
y este comienzo otoñal
pulso acelerado
y torturado corazón?
Sí
es el desamor
la vasta y ecuménica desilusión.

INSISTENCE DOES NOT SEDUCE, IT SURRENDERS

Each day has its own
meaning
and the year spins
burdened with memories

Happy is the one
who entrusts to his virtue
the crushing execution
of daily life

I have tried to
I have insisted on
But I alone
am not enough for love
between the two of us

and this growing emptiness
and this autumnal beginning
accelerated pulse
and tortured heart?
Yes
It is the lovelessness
the vast and ecumenical disillusion.

LAGUNA

Caballo del silencio
(todos los ruidos oyéndose sin ruido)
sobre las altas copas del bosque galopando

Luna de los ahogados

Hondura vertical
de suaves raíces hundidas en el agua

Ni un velero se atreve
plomos peces tan sólo traficando

LAGOON

Horse of silence
(all noises hearing themselves without noise)
galloping above the forest's high treetops

Moon of the drowned

Vertical depth
of soft roots sunk in the water

Not one sailboat dares
only lead-colored fish trafficking

RESUCITO AHORA

Innumerables cosas
                    me han sucedido
Virgen santa
apiádate de mí
Inmaculada

Como el ahogado
                    antes de sucumbir
se apoya en el fondo del mar y salta
sacando fuera
                    su cabeza exhausta
resucito ahora
mientras la muerte como el mar
mi hundimiento espera
ajena a mi lucha
ciega a tu milagro.

I AM RESUSCITATED NOW

Innumerable things
                    have happened to me
Virgin Mary
have pity on me
Immaculate

Just as he who drowned
                    before succumbing
pushed off the bottom of the sea
throwing his exhausted
                    head from the water
I am resuscitated now
While death like the sea
waits for me to sink
indifferent to my struggle
blind to your miracle.

EN MÍ Y NO ESTANDO

Siempre ausente la mirada
los ojos y el corazón
puestos en Nicaragua
en las personas que he amado
en mis hijos
en las personas que me han amado
en mi familia en Nicaragua
en los sitios donde he vivido
en lo que he soñado
en mi familia en Nicaragua
en vanos entusiasmos, ya pasados
en mis estudios, inútiles ahora
en la poesía
en mi familia en Nicaragua
en mis buenos amigos
en mis padres
en mis hermanos
en mi familia en Nicaragua
en lo que he amado
en esto y en lo otro
en lo contradictorio
en lo que he fracasado
en lo que me he empeñado
en mi familia en Nicaragua
y ausente de mí mismo estoy
con mi familia en Nicaragua.

IN ME AND FAR AWAY

I have an absent look
my eyes and my heart
are fixed on Nicaragua
on the people I love
on my children
on the people who love me
on my family in Nicaragua
on the places where I've lived
on my dreams
on my family in Nicaragua
on my wild ideas
now part of the past
on my studies
now useless
on poetry
on my family in Nicaragua
on my good friends
on my parents
on my brothers
on my family in Nicaragua
on what I've loved
on this and that
on the contradictory
on all my failures
on everything I've started
on my family in Nicaragua
and I am absent from myself
with my family in Nicaragua

EL EXILADO

Un día gané el umbral de la Embajada
jodido!, mejor me hubieran agarrado

> (y si me torturan
> y si me matan?)

Al otro día en el vuelo 501 salía
                              de mi Patria
> (Talvez otra suerte alumbre
> talvez otros pulsos latan)

Y me pasé 10 años soñando con mi casa

y se pidieron garantías
y me dieron el visado
y prometí no meterme en nada

Luego me encontré solo en medio
                              de las calles

y me pregunté desconcertado:
Pero, ¿es ésta la Patria?
            ¿es ésto lo soñado?
Y tanta miseria y tanta ignominia
¿podré quedarme sin meterme en nada?

EXILE

One day I reached the doorway of the Embassy
Shit! I might have been better off if they had grabbed me

>   (and if they torture me
>   and if they kill me?)

The other day on Flight 501 I left
>   my country
>   (Maybe my lucky star will rise
>   maybe my heart will pump new blood)

And I spent ten years dreaming about my house

and they asked me for guarantees
and they gave me a visa
and I promised not to get involved in anything

Then I found myself alone in the middle
>   of the streets

I was upset and I asked myself:
But what kind of country is this?
Is this what I dreamed about?
With such misery and disgrace
how can I stay here and not get involved?

Francisco Valle

(1942-   )

A well-forged combination of French surrealism and a concern for the indigenous Nicaragua characterizes Francisco Valle's verse and poems in prose. Valle's work contains certain affinities with Alejo Carpentier's theory of *lo real maravilloso:* the natural surrealism or super-realism that exists in Latin America creates a different reality that defies description by objective, logical means. Valle has traveled extensively in Europe and South America and translates French and English poetry.

LA DOBLE SANGRE

Las loras lloran en el guarumo, poniendo en el cielo el grito de cristal. Los chillidos brotan de la corteza, y abren mi soledad con una dormida ala de azufre. Sobre la memoria del yermo, el talismán. Huraña, brillas en la tiniebla como una cruz vegetal, y el deseo te riega de collar la entraña. En el patio de ámbito sombrío, tu frente—invitación a la luz—es una hoguera que lame el destino del estío y calcina los secretos del cielo. Yo soy la noche y duermo sobre ti.

THE DOUBLE BLOOD

The parrots call in the *guarumo* tree, placing a crystal cry in the
sky. Their shrieks sprout from the bark and open my solitude with a
sleeping wing of brimstone. Over the memory of the desert, the
talisman. Bashful, you shine in the darkness like a cross of plants.
Desire waters your heart with a necklace. In the patio's somber
space, your forehead is an invitation to light, a bonfire that licks the
summer's destiny and burns the secrets of the sky. I am the night
and I sleep upon you.

LA PIPA DE NOGAL

Toda la desolación pasó por mis labios.

En la pipa oscura de nogal, la muerte escribió, con lívida nomenclatura, la sombra de las palabras perdidas, y cada ciudad solitaria fue grabando en su cuerpo de anacoreta una profunda tajadura.

Como un ángel antiguo, la pipa soñaba en mi boca.

Como una barca silenciosa, se perdía entre las torres negras.

A medianoche, en la penumbra, resplandecía su brasa honda; a mediodía, yacía quieta, inmóvil, y su grueso vientre color de raíz fósil consolaba al mundo.

A veces, encontrada de pronto, sobre una mesa, en una gaveta, sobre un armario, la pipa —en la soledad del cuarto— tenía un silencio de otras edades, y su tristeza era una elegía de piedra que se dormía entre las manos.

Caminó mucho tiempo conmigo, hasta que ya al final —anciana renca y arruinada— perdió totalmente la mirada frente a las tinieblas del mar.

Tuve que dejarla, y ahí quedó sobre la arena, como una religión abandonada.

Yo me perdí por un camino en donde las tardes caían sobre la vida como las cenizas de los reyes muertos.

THE WALNUT PIPE

All desolation had passed by my lips.

On the dark walnut pipe, death wrote the shadow of lost words with an angry hand. Each solitary city engraved a deep cut in its ascetic body.

Like an antique angel, the pipe dreamed in my mouth.

Like a silent ship, it lost itself among black towers.

At midnight its ember glowed in the darkness. At noon it was quiet, immobile. Its belly, the color of petrified roots, consoled the world.

Sometimes, in the solitude of the room, when I found it suddenly on a table, a dresser, or in a drawer, the pipe had a silence of other ages. Its sadness was an elegy of stone sleeping between hands.

It journeyed a long time with me, until finally—ancient, lame and ruined—it totally lost its gaze before the darkness of the sea.

I had to leave it, and there it remained on the sand like an abandoned religion.

I got lost on a path where the afternoons were falling on life like the ashes of dead kings.

MUJER Y TIGRE

El tigre camina sobre tu pecho, y oye el canto de tu corazón, como el resonar de un cáliz golpeado con el nudoso gonce de un dedo.

En la sala vacía, sin nadie—porque es una semana compuesta de siete domingos secos—caminas con el lamento del mar en las pupilas, y en la comba de la cintura, el vello ralo, espesándose por la ternura baja del vientre, se apiña en el vértice como un sufrimiento de renegridos destellos que baja reposando sobre la piedra del consuelo.

Todo se acerca a tí, desde la música hasta el ángel, porque en tus labios de agua se mecen las canoas.

WOMAN AND TIGER

The tiger walks on your chest and hears the song of your heart like the echoing of a chalice struck with the knotted hinge of a finger.

There is no one in the empty chamber because it is a week composed of seven dry Sundays. You walk there with the lament of the sea in your pupils. On the curve of your waist, the sparse down thickens below the loving belly and crowds into the vertex: the black flashes of suffering descend and come to rest on the stone of consolation.

All things draw near to you, from the music to the angel, because on your lips of water the canoes are rocking.

INVIERNO

Invierno
Yo te dejara mi boca azul junto a la piedra donde cayó el cacique
Junto al guayabo de fuego
Llevando en alto una lanza y rezando antes de perderme en el
*   torbellino*

Invierno
Esta manada es la más dura por las coronas
La pulsera en el pie y la flauta en el crepúsculo
El hueso tapado con cinco dedos
Y el viento se escucha lejano como si soplaran en un caracol

Invierno
Ronca sobre mí Dá vueltas
Acompaña estos desolados versos que bocabajo lloran en los
*   caminos*
Y que al escampar sea mi cuerpo música tierra mojada perfume
*   de la tarde*

WINTER

Winter
I would leave you my blue mouth next to the stone where the leader
    of the tribe fell
next to the guava of fire
as he lifted a spear and prayed before losing me in the whirlwind

Winter
This herd is the hardest because of the crowns
The bracelet on the ankle and the flute in the dusk
The bone covered with five fingers
And the wind one hears from far away as if they were blowing into a
    conch

Winter
Roar above me Toss and turn
Accompany this desolate poem that cries on the paths with downturned
    mouth
And when the skies clear let my body be music wet land afternoon
    perfume

EN SILENCIO

¿Quién se mete en el agua
    abajo
de la noche y el cacho
de la vaca tornasoleando rayos?

¿Quién se acuesta en el puente
    cansado
mientras en el río saltan los peces
    chatos
de cólera y amarillos de hieles?

Yo me acuesto en el puente para jamás despertar
y me hundo en el agua
y me hundo en la sombra que me abandonará en el mar

IN SILENCE

Who gets in the water
beneath the night and the horn
of the iridescent bull?

Who falls asleep on the bridge
while in the river
the snub-nosed fish
leap yellow as bile?

I fall asleep on the bridge
never to wake again
and I submerge myself
in the water and in the shadow
that will abandon me in the sea.

Ana Ilce

(1945-   )

The growing number of women poets in Nicaragua had two
accomplished precursors: María Teresa Sánchez (1918) and
Mariana Sansón Argüello (1918). The ample base of the Nicara-
guan revolution in terms of the participation of women is reflected
in the upsurge of activist-poets such as Michele Najlis (1945) and
Gioconda Belli (1948), winner of the *Casa de las Américas* prize
in 1978 for her book, *Línea de fuego*. Pablo Antonio Cuadra says
the following about Ana Ilce and her book, *Las ceremonias del
silencio:* "Below, on earth, [she is] the spinner of love. Above, in
the nocturnal workshop, the weaver of myth. The reader will find
her...where the lover is deceived as he looks for her. On the
"Sacrificial Stone". Executioner and victim...Reading herself her
sentence, woman to woman. But saving herself from her scaffold,
poem to poem."

CALLE DE VERANO

La tarde seca arañando los tejados.
Dos niños que brincan en medio del remolino de polvo
    anaranjado.
Una sombra como de anciana que pasa
dejando un viento de tristeza.
El tiempo que transcurre.
El alma que se pone del color de la tierra.
La tarde que se encorva como un arco
por donde pasan los niños
tomados de las manos de sus madres.
La lluvia que no cae.
Sólo la cal del aire que blanquea las sienes.
Sólo el fuego que penetra en la sangre y que tiñe
de amarillo los ojos.
Sólo la vida como un animal muerto
tendido bajo el cielo.
Y el sol secando al aire las médulas cárdenas del tiempo.
Y el viento lúgubre, estepario.
Y los pasos pesados.
Y los niños ya viejos regresando bajo el arco de la tarde.
Y las piedras.

SUMMER STREET

The dry afternoon scraping the rooftops.
Two children skipping in a whirlpool of orange dust.
A shadow like an old woman passing by
leaving a wind of sadness.
The time that elapses.
The soul that turns the color of the earth.
The afternoon that bends over like an arch
through which the children pass
taken by their mothers' hands.
The rain that does not fall.
Only the ashen air that whitens the forehead.
Only the fire that penetrates the blood and dyes
the eyes yellow.
Only the life like a dead animal
stretched out beneath the sky.
And in the air the sun drying the black-and-blue marrow of time.
And the dismal wind from the vast plain.
And the heavy steps.
And the children already old returning beneath the arch of the
    afternoon.
And the stones.

FURIOSOS PÁJAROS

Estos son los furiosos pájaros
del deseo.
Ellos son negros.
Ellos se mueven sin hacerles
una señal determinada.

Un día los ví venir con sigilo,
con sorna,
con prisa en sus oscuras patas.
Ahora los veo pasar

—¡Negros y eternos pájaros!—
reconociéndome
y saludándome.

FURIOUS BIRDS

These are the furious birds
of desire.
They are black.
They move without making
a definite sign.

One day I saw them come secretly,
cunningly,
hurrying on their dark feet.
Now I see them pass by

—Black and eternal birds!—
recognizing me
and greeting me.

LETRA VIVA

Vamos en viaje con la vida. Todos adultos y yo como pollo recién salido de la cáscara. Venimos de un punto harto verdadero a errar sobre esta calle imaginaria. Y no, no resucitaremos como Lázaro. Atrás el profeta, la sibila délfica, y el nigromante porque sólo ha de triunfar la zarpa y el dentellazo puro de la muerte. Entre tanto a mí dénme el reposo, el hosco sello de mujer con el hombro que sostenga la poronga de agua nueva y recién hecha. Que al fin y al cabo, nuestro único dominio será ésto: El horror a la fosa común, la espalda inadecuada para el golpe que nos ha de partir.

LIVING WORDS

We journey with life. All adults, and I like a newly-hatched chicken. We came from such a true point to wander on this imaginary street. And no, we will not rise from the dead like Lazarus. Behind us, the prophet, the delphic sybil, and the necromancer because only the claw and the pure fangs of death will triumph. Until then, let me rest like the dark woman with the vessel of new, freshly-made water on her shoulder. Finally, at the end, our sole dominion will be this: the horror of the common grave, the back inadequate to the blow that will split us open.

Álvaro Urtecho

(1951-   )

Alvaro Urtecho's poetry draws heavily from the literature of the Spanish Renaissance and Baroque periods, especially the meditative and philosophical poetry of Fray Luis de León. Modern poets such as Rainer Maria Rilke, Wallace Stevens and Carlos Martínez Rivas have also had a significant impact on Urtecho's largely unpublished body of work. Urtecho studied philosophy for five years in Spain, continued his studies in Costa Rica, and is now teaching in Managua.

LÁZARO

El seco estrépito
de un repentino alzarse de palomas
estremeció mis pasos.

Fue como si algo
se me escapara de la carne,
sorprendida su raíz.

Como si al muerto que guardo
le levantaran la losa y por el mundo
caminara ya sin nada entre las manos.

LAZARUS

The dry uproar
of a sudden lifting of doves
shook my steps.

As if something
had escaped from my flesh,
its root surprised.

As if they lifted the slab from the corpse
I guard and through the world
it journeyed now with nothing in its hands.

CONSOLACIÓN DEL FUEGO

No sé qué grandes angustias
me producen estos días de inmolaciones
y lejanías cargadas de frío
y palabras no halladas
que quizá se pudrieron en el murmullo amarillo
del otoño.

No sé qué se escapó en la niebla
la noche en que creí ver a Dios agazapado
viviendo aún,
                    y creí oír el poema,
y era sólo el espacio con bujías blancas
ante las puertas de la ciudad interminable,
sin nombre ya,
como en los cuentos grises de algún
Maelstrom.

No sé qué rostros crueles me acechan.
Ni sé por qué las nieves inocentes
me fustigan como inesperado infierno,
y el mundo se detiene así,
                              como una vez ayer,
o siempre,
habitado por desolados cantos.

CONSOLATION OF THE FIRE

I do not know what great anguish
they produced in me—these days of immolations
and distances burdened with cold
and undiscovered words
that perhaps decayed in the yellow murmur
of Autumn.

I do not know what escaped in the fog
the night I thought I saw God, hidden
but still alive.
                    I thought I heard the poem
and it was only the space with white candles
before the gates of the interminable city,
now unnamed,
like the gray stories of some
Maelstrom.

I do not know what cruel faces watch me.
Nor do I know why the innocent snow
whips me like an unforeseen hell
and the world stops this way,
like yesterday at one time,
or always,
inhabited by desolate songs.

GRUTA

Húmedos labios enmudecen cuando
en el fondo de un cuarto los amantes
desnudos sonríen, acarician, contemplan,
agrandan la sombra donde el amor
y la muerte no tienen ya nada que temerse.

GROTTO

Moist lips grow silent when
at the bottom of a room the naked
lovers smile, caress, contemplate,
enlarge the shadow where love
and death no longer have anything to fear.

BENDICIÓN

Y qué podemos decir de la lluvia que regocijada
   lame los cristales de tu cuarto,
ahora que la noche nos interna más y más
   entre las vértebras,
y un solo gemido apaga finalmente las palabras
   en la penumbra insólita del gozo.

Ahora que mis manos, ya calmadas,
   van bordeando lentamente
las tuyas, hasta casi asirlas;
   ahora que el corazón se calla, agradecido,
y los cuerpos yacen uno
   junto al otro, sin apenas notarlo;

con los ojos muy abiertos hacia arriba,
   ¿qué podemos pedirle al cielo
sino la persistencia de esta lluvia
   que afuera cae sorda, voraz, empecinada?

BLESSING

And what can we say about the rain
      that licks the windows of your room with pleasure,
now that the night hides us deeper and deeper
      among the vertebrae,
and a single moan finally extinguishes the words
      in the strange, half-darkness of joy.

My hands, calm now,
      slowly reach for yours
and almost grasp them.
Now that the heart is silent, grateful,
      and the bodies lie one
next to the other, scarcely aware of it;

with wide-open eyes staring upward,
      what can we ask of the sky
but the persistence of this rain
      that falls outside, deaf, voracious, stubborn?

SÁBADO A MEDIODÍA

Azorado, ceñido el corazón a sus imágenes,
frente al intenso resplandor del sol
que se endurece entre el tejado de zinc
y los cables del alumbrado público,
piensa en la ciudad en que ahora vive
y se sabe, como en todas, extranjero.
Piensa en la lentitud del mundo,
la lentitud soberbia del mundo
y las cosas rotundas que ha visto.
Símbolos, seres, signos. Todo tan real:
el paso de los años, el rito de los hijos
enterrando a sus padres, tántos
cuerpos amados, sus bocas olvidadas,
la dulzura del niño perdido, el fragor,
el oscuro designio, la incandescencia...
Reclama un horizonte que no lo petrifique
una patria florida y generosa que dé amor
a sus hijos, un color, un movimiento
para la imaginación.
                      Cree que hay un lugar
donde él iría, un oculto lugar en un bosque.
Se siente allí, se imagina una senda esencial:
una cierta vereda con muy pocas figuras
en la bruma lechosa, un breve cementerio,
una fronda cercana de ondulados rumores
y ladridos y voces y campanas fluyendo
de otros tiempos como sangre...
                      Se sabe
tenebroso, es cierto, y siente
como le crece por dentro la condena.

SATURDAY AT NOON

Perplexed, the heart fitted to its images,
before the intense brilliance of the sun
that grows harder between the corrugated metal roof
and the cables of the street lights,
he thinks of this city where he lives now
feeling foreign to them all.
He considers the slowness of the world,
the arrogant slowness of the world
and all the round things he has seen.
Symbols, beings, signs. Everything so real:
the passage of years, rituals of sons
burying their fathers and so many
bodies loved and then their mouths forgotten,
the sweetness of the lost child, the clamor
the obscure design, the incandescence...
He claims a horizon that does not petrify him,
a generous country in bloom giving love
to its children, a color, a movement
for the imagination.
                              He believes there is a place
where he could go, a hidden place of trees.
There he imagines himself on some essential path:
a certain trail with only a few figures
in the milky fog, a brief graveyard,
the foliage nearby of rippling whispers
and barking and voices and bells flowing
from other times like blood...
                              He feels
tenebrous, to be sure, and knows
how from within the condemnation grows.

ERRATA

Page	For	Read
203, line 9	Madellín	Medellín
	Antioquía	Antioquia
13	Culture	Cultura
28	Direction	Directions
29	'	&
31	Pole	Pol
38	Impren	Imprenta
204, line 6	Editions	Editiones
16	1049	1949
31	A(vila	Avila
33	Andreita	Andreíta
40	rosros	rostros
205, line 5	Milo	Hilo
9	managua	Managua
16	Managa	Managua
23	Guaranía	Guarania
206, line 9	higas	hijas
12	Píndero	Pindaro
	ultura	Cultura
15	Selve	Selva
21	amanecar	amanecer
31	conemporánea	contemporánea
207, line 12	Carcía	García
13	Alfera	Alfaro
20	Academica	Academia
29	muera	nueva
36	fanguar-	vanguar-
39	quirón	Quirón
208, line 3	Farias, Victor	Farías, Víctor
	Aravcaria	Araucaria
5	Sepember	September

Selective Bibliography

Cardenal, Ernesto. "La ciudad deshabitada." *Cuadernos Americanos*, XXV, No. 1 (1946), pp. 211-219.

———. "El conquistador." *Revista de Guatemala*, (1947).

———. "Hora O." *Revista Mexicana de Literatura*, (1959).

———. *Gethsemani, Ky*. Prologue by Thomas Merton. México: Ediciones Ecuador, 1960.

———. *Epigramas*. Mexico: Universidad Nacional Autónoma de México, 1961; rpt. Buenos Aires: Carlos Lohlé, 1972.

———. *Salmos*. Madellín: Universidad de Antioquía, 1964.

———. *Oración por Marilyn Monroe y otros poemas*. Medellín: Ediciones la Tertulia, 1965.

———. *El estrecho dudoso*. Prologue by José Coronel Urtecho. Madrid: Ediciones Culture Hispánica, 1966.

———. *Antología*. Santiago, Chile: Impresora Horizonte, 1967.

———. *Mayapán*. Managua: Ediciones de Librería Cardenal, 1968.

———. *Homenaje a los indios americanos*. León, Nicaragua: Editorial Universitaria, 1969; rpt. Santiago, Chile: Editorial Universitaria, 1970.

———. *La hora O y otros poemas*. Barcelona: El Bardo, 1971.

———. *Canto nacional*. Mexico: Siglo XXI, 1973.

———. *Oráculo sobre Managua*. Buenos Aires: Ediciones Carlos Lohlé, 1973.

———. *Poesía escogida*. Barcelona: Barral Editores, 1974.

TRANSLATIONS INTO ENGLISH (BOOKS)

———. *Homage to the American Indians*. Trans. Monique Carlos Altschul. Baltimore: Johns Hopkins University Press, 1973.

———. *Marilyn Monroe and Other Poems*. Trans. by Robert Pring-Mill. London: Search Press, 1975.

———. *Apocalypse & Other Poems*. Ed. Robert Pring-Mill and Donald D. Walsh. New York: New Direction, 1977.

———. *Zero Hour ' Other Documentary Poems*. Ed. Donald D. Walsh. Trans. Paul W. Borgeson and Jonathan Cohen. New York: New Directions, 1980.

Coronel Urtecho, José. *Pole-la d'ananta ḳatanta paranta. Imitaciones y traducciones*. León: Editorial Universitaria, 1970.

Cortés, Alfonso. *La odisea del istmo*. Guatemala: Tip. Latina, 1922.

———. *Poesías*. Managua: Imprenta Nacional, 1931; rpt. Managua: Editorial Hospicio, 1931.

———. *Tardes de oro*. León: Tip. de J. Hernández, 1934.

———. *Poemas eleusinos*. León: Talleres del Hospicio San Juan de Dios, 1935.

———. *Las siete antorchas del sol*. León: Impren a Hospicio, 1952.

———. *30 poemas de Alfonso*. Managua: El Hilo Azul, 1952.

_____. Las rimas universales. Prologue by Thomas Merton. Managua: Editorial Alemana, 1964.

_____. Las coplas del pueblo. Managua: Editorial Alemana, 1965.

_____. Las Puertas del pasatiempo. Managua: Editorial Alemana, 1967.

_____. El poema cotidiano. León: Editorial Hospicio, 1967.

_____. Treinta poemas. Managua: Edicions de Librería Cardenal, 1968.

_____. Poemas. San José, Costa Rica: Educa, 1971.

Cuadra, Pablo Antonio. Canciones de pájaro y señora. Unpublished: 1929-1931: appeared in part in Poesía. Madrid. Ediciones Cultura Hispánica, 1964.

_____. Poemas nicaragüenses. Santiago, Chile: Editorial Nascimento, 1934.

_____. Canto temporal. Granada, Nicaragua: Ediciones Cuadernos del Taller San Lucas, 1943.

_____. Libro de horas. Published in Antología de la Poesía católica del siglo XX. Madrid: A. Vasallo, 1964; rpt. in Poesía.

_____. Poemas con un crepúsculo a cuestas. Published in part in Cuadernos Hispanoamericanos. No. 10 (1949). Published in its entirety in Poesía.

_____. La tierra prometida. Selección de poemas. Managua: Editorial El Hilo Azul, 1952.

_____. Elegías. Mallorca: Papeles de Son Armadans, 1957.

_____. El jaguar y la luna. Illustrated by the author. Managua: Editoral Artes Gráficas, 1959; rpt. Buenos Aires: Ediciones Carlos Lohlé, 1971.

_____. Zoo. San Salvador: Dirección Gral. de Publicaciones, Ministerio de Educación, 1962.

_____. Poesía. Selección 1929-1962. Madrid: Ediciones Cultura Hispánica, 1964.

_____. "Noche de América para un poeta español." Cuadernos Hispanoamericanos, No. 187-188 (1965).

_____. Personae. Mallorca: Papeles de Son Armadans No. 146, 1968.

_____. Poesía escogida. León: Editorial Universitaria, 1968.

_____. Los cantos de Cifar. Mallorca: Papeles de Son Armadans No. 156, 1969.

_____. Nuevos cantos de Cifar. Mallorca: Papelas de Son Armadans No. 181, 1971.

_____. Cantos de Cifar. A('vila, Spain: Editorial El Toro de Granito, Institución Gran Duque de Alba, 1971.

_____. Doña Andreita y otros retratos. Caracas: Ediciones Poesía de Venezuela, 1971.

_____. Mayo. Oráculo de los cuatro héroes. Managua: Editorial Asel, 1974.

_____. Tierra que habla. Antología. San José, Costa Rica: Educa, 1974; 2nd ed., 1977.

_____. Apocalipsis con figuras—Managua/72. Madrid: La Estafeta Literaria No. 77, 1977.

_____. Esos rosros que asoman en la multitud. Managua: Ediciones El Pez y la Serpiente, 1976.

_____. Cantos de Cifar y de la mar dulce. Managua: Ediciones Academia Nicaragüense de la Lengua, 1979.

_____. Siete árboles contra el atardecer. Caracas: Ediciones de la Presidencia de la República, 1980.

_____. *The Jaguar and the Moon.* Trans. Thomas Merton. Greensboro: Unicorn Press, 1974.

_____. *Songs of Cifar and the Sweet Sea.* Trans. and Ed. Grace Schulman and Ann McCarthy de Zavala. New York: Columbia University Press, 1979.

Gutiérrez, Ernesto. *Yo conocía algo hace tiempo.* Managua: Editorial El Milo Azul, 1953.

_____. *Años bajo el sol.* Managua: Ediciones El Pez y la Serpiente, 1963.

_____. *Terrestre celeste.* León: Editorial Universitaria, 1969.

_____. *Poemas políticos.* Prologue by Ernesto Cardenal. managua: Editorial Unión, 1970.

_____. *Temas de la Hélade.* Madrid: Ediciones Cultura Hispánica, 1973.

_____. *Antología poética.* Selection by Carlos Martínez Rivas and Sergio Ramírez. San José, Costa Rica: Educa, 1976.

Gutiérrez, Juan Francisco. *Tú, mi residencia.* Madrid: Colección el Barco de Papel, 1952.

_____. *La libertad y el amor.* Managa: Editorial Nicaragüense, 1962.

_____. *Elegía a la muerte de un presidente.* With a translation by Thomas Merton. New York: Editorial Hispana, 1966.

_____. *Tantos años y siempre.* Unpublished.

_____. *Vita ego te absolvo. Antología personal.* Unpublished.

Ilce, Ana. *Las ceremonias del silencio.* Managua: Ediciones El Pez y la Serpiente, 1975.

Martínez Rivas, Carlos. *La insurrección solitaria.* México: Editorial Guaranía, 1953; rpt. San José, Costa Rica: Educa, 1973.

_____. "Dos Murales U.S.A." *Cuadernos Hispanoamericanos,* No. 181, (1964).

_____. *Calcoholmanias.* Unpublished.

_____. *Allegro Irato.* Two volumes. Unpublished.

Mejía Sánchez, Ernesto. "Ensalmos y conjuros." *Cuadernos Americanos, VII,* No. 1 (1948) pp. 211-214.

_____. *La carne contigua.* Buenos Aires: Ediciones Sur, 1948.

_____. *El retorno.* México: Ediciones Los Presentes, 1950.

_____. *La impureza.* Premio Nacional Rubén Darío, 1951. Unpublished.

_____. *Contemplaciones europeas.* San Salvador: Ministerio de Cultura, Departamento Editorial, 1957.

_____. *Poemas.* Buenos Aires: 1963.

_____. *Prosemas del sur y de Levante.* Málaga: 1968.

_____. *Recolección.* León: Editorial Universitaria, 1972.

Pasos Joaquín. *Breve suma*. Managua: Edtorial Nuevos Horizontes, 1945.

_____. *Poemas de un joven*. México: Fondo de Cultura Económica, 1962.

_____. *Joaquín Pasos 1914-1947*. León: Cuadernos Universitarios No. 7, 1972.

de la Selva, Salomón. *11 Poems of Rubén Darío*. Trans. Thomas Walsh and Salomón de la Selva. New York: Hispanic Society of America, 1916.

_____. *Tropical Town and Other Poems*. New York: John Lane, 1918.

_____. *El soldado desconocido*. México: Cultura, 1922; rpt. San José, Costa Rica: Educa, 1971.

_____. *Las higas de Erechteo*. unpublished. 1933.

_____. *Evocación de Horacio*. Unpublished. 1949.

_____. *Canto a la independencia de México*. México: 1955.

_____. *Evocación de Píndero*. San Salvador: Ministerio de ultura, Departamento Editorial, 1957.

_____. *Acomixtli Netzahualcoyotl*. unpublished. 1958.

_____. *Homenaje a Salomón de la Selve*. León: Cuadernos Universitarios No. 5, 1969.

_____. *Versos y versiones nobles y sentimentales*. Managua: Banco de América, 1974.

Urtecho, Alvaro. *Tumba y residencia*. Unpublished.

_____. *Cantata estupefacta*. Unpublished.

Valle, Francisco. *Casi al amanecar*. México: Ediciones Cuadernos del Viento, 1964.

_____. *Laberinto de espadas*. Managua: Tip. Morgantheler, 1974.

_____. "Luna entra ramas." *El Pez y la Serpiente*, No. 19 (1978).

_____. "La puerta secreta." *Forja*, No. 52 (1979).

USEFUL ANTHOLOGIES

Cuadra Downing, Orlando. *Nueva poesía nicaragüense*. Madrid: Seminario de Problemas Hispanoamericanos, 1949.

"Poesía de Nicaragua." *El Corno Emplumado*, Ed. Margaret Randall and Sergio Mondragón, No. 3 (1962) pp. 60-68.

"Poesía nicaragüense conemporánea." *El Corno Emplumado*, No. 15 (1965) pp. 35-72.

Gutiérrez, Ernesto. *Poesía nicaragüense post-dariana*. León: Cuadernos Universitarios No. 3, 1967.

Nueva antología de la poesía nicaragüense. Managua: Ediciones El Pez y la Serpiente, 1972.

Cardenal, Ernesto. *Poesía nicaragüense*. Havana: Casa de las Américas, 1973; rpt. Buenos Aires: Ediciones Carlos Lohlé, 1973; and San José, Costa Rica: Ediciones El Pez y la Serpiente, 1976.

Nicaragua in Revolution: the Poets Speak, A Bilingual Collage. Ed. Bridget Aldaraca, Edward Baker, Ileana Rodriguez and Marc Zimmerman, Minneapolis: Marxist Educational Press, 1980.

USEFUL STUDIES

BOOKS

Arellano, Jorge Eduardo. *Panorama de la literatura nicaragüense*. Managua: Ediciones Nacionales, 1977, 3rd revised edition.

_____. *El movimento de vanguardia de Nicaragua, 1927-1932*. Managua: Imprenta Novedades, 1969; rpt. Managua: Ediciones de Librería Cultural Nicaragüense, 1971.

Coronel Urtecho, José. *Prosa*. San José, Costa Rica: Educa, 1972.

Darío, Rubén. *Bibliografía general de Rubén Darío*. Ed. José Jirón Terán. León: Cuadernos Universitarios, 1967.

_____. *Selected Poems*. Trans. Lysander Kemp. Prologue by Octavio Paz from "El caracol y la sirena." *Cuadrivio*. Mexico: Joaquín Mortiz, 1965. Austin: University of Texas Press, 1965. (Also includes "A Speech Al Alimón on Rubén Darío" by Pablo Neruda and Federico Carcía Lorca, PEN Club, Buenos Aires, 1933).

Guardia de Alfera, Gloria. *El pensamiento poético de Pablo Antonio Cuadra*. Madrid: Editorial Gredos, 1971.

Merton, Thomas. *Emblems of a Season of Fury*. Norfolk, Conn.: New Directions, 1963.

Morales, Beltrán. *Sin páginas amarillas*. Managua: Ediciones Nacionales, 1975.

Varela-Ibarra, José L. *La poesía de Alfonso Cortés*. León: Editorial Universitaria, 1977.

Ycaza Tijerino, Julio. La Poesía y los poetas de Nicaragua. Managua: Academica Nicaragüense de la Lengua, 1958.

Ernesto Cardenal, poeta de la liberación latinoamericana. Buenos Aires: Fernando García Cambeiro, 1975.

ESSAYS

Baciu, Stefan. "Pablo Antonio Cuadra, poeta de Hispanoamérica." *La Estafeta Literaria*, June (1966).

Cardenal, Ernesto. "Joaquín Pasos: un joven que no ha viajado nunca." *Cuadernos Americanos*, VI, No. 4 (1947) pp. 224-232.

_____. "Ansias y lengua de la muera poesía nicaragüense." in *Nueva poesía nicaragüense*. Ed. Orlando Cuadra Downing. Madrid: Seminario de Problemas Hispanoamericanos, 1949, pp. 7-99.

_____. "Alfonso Cortés." *Revista Conservadora del Pensamiento Centroamericano*, No. 101 (1969) pp. 27-32.

_____. "Lo que fue Solentiname. Carta al pueblo de Nicaragua." *Casa de las Américas*, No. 108 (1978) pp. 158-160.

Cuadra, Pablo Antonio. "Los poetas en la torre (memorias del movimiento de fanguardia)." in *Torres de Dios*. Managua: Ediciones de la Academia Nicaragüense de la Lengua, 1958, pp. 143-208.

_____. "Alfonso, discípulo del Centauro quirón." *Revista Conservadora del Pensamiento Centroamericano*, No. 101 (1969) pp. 24-26.

Dorfman, Ariel. "Ernesto Cardenal: *!Todo el poder a Dios Proleteriado!" in *Ensayos quemados en Chile, inocencia y neo-colonialismo*, Buenos Aires: Ediciones de la Flor, 1974, pp. 193-223.

207

_____. "Tiempo de amor, tiempo de lucha: la unidad en los *Epigramas de Ernesto Cardenal*." *Texto Crítico,* Year v, No. 13 (1979) pp. 3-44.

Farias, Victor. "La poesía de Ernesto Cardenal." *Araucaria,* 15 (1981) pp. 101-118.

de la Selva, Salomón. "Rubén Darío." *Poetry: A Magazine of Verse,* vol. VIII, April-Sepember (1916) pp. 200-204.

Valle, Francisco. "La poesía de Pablo Antonio Cuadra." *Poesía Española,* CLV, November (1965).

White, Steven F. "Toward Cultural Dialogue with Nicaragua." *Third Rail,* No. 5 (1982).

Biographical Note

Steven F. White was born in Abington, Pennsylvania in 1955 and was raised in Glencoe, Illinois. He received a B.A. in English from Williams College and an M.A. in Spanish and Hispanic American literature from the University of Oregon. His awards include the Academy of American Poets Prize in 1975 and 1977 as well as the Hubbard Hutchinson Fellowship from Williams College which enabled him to travel and to work in various Latin American countries for two years. His poems and translations have appeared in numerous magazines including *Review* (Center for Inter-American Relations), *New Directions Anthology, Nicaraguan Perspectives, Aspen Anthology, La Prensa Libre* (San José, Costa Rica), *La Prensa Literaria* (Managua, Nicaragua), and *Anthology of Magazine Verse & Yearbook of American Poetry.* Mr. White is presently living in Nicaragua.

Grace Shulman's book of poems, *Burn Down the Icons,* was published by Princeton University Press. Her poems, essays and translations have appeared in many publications, including *The New Yorker, Hudson Review, American Poetry Review, Poetry, Antaeus* and *The Georgia Review.* She has been Poetry Editor of *The Nation* since May, 1972, and Director of The Poetry Center, 92nd Street YM-YWHA since January, 1974. A former Vice-President of P. E. N., she is an Associate Professor at Baruch College, C. U. N. Y., and holds a Ph. D. from New York University. She is editor of *Ezra Pound: A Collection of Criticism* (McGraw), and co-translator of *Songs of Cifar and the Sweet Sea,* by Pablo Antonio Cuadra (Columbia University Press). She is the recipient of a Witter Bynner Grant-in-Aid for her translation of T. Carmi's *At the Stone of Losses.*